Praise for *Without a Net*

"An engrossing story of one woman's spiral downward . . . to homeless mother of three. [Kennedy's] observations on how much more expensive it is to be poor than rich . . . shadow Ehrenreich's, but are tinged with a visceral anxiety. Such reflections are especially salient now with Republican leaders lobbying hard to shift the tax burden from income to consumption, a move that would disproportionately penalize families in Kennedy's position."
—*The New York Times Book Review*

"Refreshingly candid . . . *Without a Net* shows how frighteningly easy it can be for an ordinary, nonsubstance-abusing middle-class woman and devoted mother to find herself unable to afford a place to live."
—*Los Angeles Times Book Review*

"Reading this book's engaging prose, one cannot help but alternate between anger and total empathy for the narrator/author. (Maybe it can happen to anyone after all.)"
—*The Washington Post Book World*

"[Kennedy's] sense of humor, ingenuity, and refreshing refusal to blame others for her mistakes won me over, and I quickly found myself rooting for her to succeed."
—*Elle*

"Kennedy's vivid account of her months of homelessness makes a lively read." —*Entertainment Weekly*

"You'd think it'd take a while to go from 'given every opportunity, spoiled in every way middle-class housewife . . . to homeless single mother,' but Kennedy did it in less than a year. . . . Once readers learn the details, the story of Kennedy's downfall goes from being unlikely to horribly plausible."
—*Publishers Weekly*

PENGUIN BOOKS

WITHOUT A NET

Michelle Kennedy's work has appeared in *The New York Times*, *Redbook*, *Family Circle*, Salon.com, and *The Christian Science Monitor*, and has been aired on NPR.

Without a Net

Middle Class and Homeless
(with Kids) in America

Michelle Kennedy

Penguin Books

To Matt, Lydia, and Alex,
who kept me from sinking into the abyss,
And to John and Liam,
who helped me reach for the light above it.

PENGUIN BOOKS
Published by the Penguin Group
Penguin Group (USA) Inc., 375 Hudson Street, New York, New York 10014, U.S.A.
Penguin Group (Canada), 90 Eglinton Avenue East, Suite 700, Toronto,
Ontario, Canada M4P 2Y3 (a division of Pearson Penguin Canada Inc.)
Penguin Books Ltd, 80 Strand, London WC2R 0RL, England
Penguin Ireland, 25 St. Stephen's Green, Dublin 2, Ireland (a division of Penguin Books Ltd)
Penguin Books Australia Ltd, 250 Camberwell Road, Camberwell, Victoria 3124, Australia
(a division of Pearson Australia Group Pty Ltd)
Penguin Books India Pvt Ltd, 11 Community Centre, Panchsheel Park, New Delhi – 110 017, India
Penguin Group (NZ), cnr Airborne and Rosedale Roads, Albany, Auckland 1310,
New Zealand (a division of Pearson New Zealand Ltd)
Penguin Books (South Africa) (Pty) Ltd, 24 Sturdee Avenue, Rosebank,
Johannesburg 2196, South Africa

Penguin Books Ltd, Registered Offices: 80 Strand, London WC2R 0RL, England

First published in the United States of America by Viking Penguin,
a member of Penguin Group (USA) Inc. 2005
Published in Penguin Books 2006

3   5   7   9   10   8   6   4

Copyright © Michelle Kennedy, 2005
All rights reserved

Brief portions of this work appeared in *The New York Times* as
"Good at Her Job, She Walked Away."

THE LIBRARY OF CONGRESS HAS CATALOGED THE HARDCOVER EDITION AS FOLLOWS:
Kennedy, Michelle.
Without a net : middle class and homeless (with kids) in America / Michelle Kennedy.
p.   cm.
ISBN 0-670-03366-9 (hc.)
ISBN 0 14 30.3678 5 (pbk.)
1. Kennedy, Michelle.   2. Mothers—United States—Biography.
3. Homeless families—United States.   I. Title.
CT275.K458525A3   2005
306.874'3'092—dc22
[B]   2004043081

Printed in the United States of America

Acknowledgments

Gratitude is an insufficient word to describe it, but many thanks to: Patty Moosbrugger, Karen Murphy, Lexy Bloom, Molly Barton, and everyone at Viking. I would never have found the courage to write the book without Tom Brooker, Warren Bluhm, Molly DeCleene, and Amy Van Beek. I would also like to thank my parents, who have always been there for me, whether I chose to admit it or not. And my husband, John Hogan, who didn't know what he was getting himself into, but stayed anyway.

Without a Net

Prologue

The click of the door handle seems entirely too loud as I pull open the door to check the breathing of my three sleeping children. They look so peaceful, sleeping there in the back of my station wagon under the yellowy light of a flickering street lamp.

I smooth the curls on Lydia's scarred face and gently close the door. Those scars—they are just one of the reasons I am seeing my children to sleep in my car. Walking through the backdoor of the kitchen, I look back once and then; all right, just once more. I smile at the cooks as I rush through the kitchen and grab the food for my customers from under the warmers. They'll keep an eye out the door for me.

It's after 1:00 A.M. when my last table leaves. I thought they would never finish. Oh, to have that kind of time to linger over a meal. It's been so long since I've had that kind of freedom. I carefully place the wineglasses in the bus tub next to the dessert plates and haul it all down the stairs. My mother would tell me to make more than one trip, but I'd always rather make one long, painful trip than two or three.

I tip out the bartender and head for the small parking lot behind the restaurant, where, I am told, my children are still blissfully asleep. I realize that I am tiptoeing my way out to the car, which makes no sense at all. I carefully open the car door and sink into the front seat. I let my head fall onto the steering wheel. I am so tired.

I am home.

"Hi, Mom," I hear from behind me. Startled, I whip around to find Matthew, the oldest, who is all of five, blinking his eyes awake.

"How was work?" he asks.

"It was fine," I reply. "Very busy. It's late though—you should go back to sleep. We'll talk in the morning."

"OK," he says, and within seconds he is out again, snuggled up against Alex, who is just fourteen months old. Living in the car doesn't seem to faze any of them in the slightest. Oh sure, they ask why we have to keep sleeping in the car, but the answer seems to suffice, and they don't whine about not having a television. Well, we do have a television, actually. It was a graduation present years before, and it's tucked in front of the passenger seat. I tried to sell it, but it wasn't worth much, so I decided to keep it. A last vestige of middle-class life, if you will. I was a middle-class housewife once upon a time. . . .

Making the leap from given-every-opportunity, spoiled-in-every-way middle-class child to boring, middle-class housewife and eventually to homeless single mother should be harder than it is. In reality, it doesn't take much more than a series of bad judgment calls and wrong decisions that, at the time, appear to be perfectly reasonable and in most cases for the better.

My own journey into homelessness did not begin with drug use, alcoholism, or any of the other things we, as a society, so often attribute to such a downward spiral. Instead, I followed my bliss right into the back of a Subaru station wagon.

At eighteen, I was a promising freshman at American University in Washington, D.C. At nineteen, I was married and pregnant with my first child. By the time I was twenty-five, I had three children and within a year, I was separated from my husband and living out of the backseat of my car, my three children all under the age of six.

This is the story of how we were homeless while I simultaneously tried to hide it from my family, my friends, and the rest of the world. By day, I walked the streets of Stone Harbor, Maine, as the completely normal mother of three children, looking in shop windows and going to the library and the Laundromat. By night, however, I was driving around town, looking for a place to park and sleep, bathing at the truck stop, and boiling ramen noodle dinners on public grills.

I had a decent job waiting tables and, although I did my best to hide my situation, I found that revealing myself, even in small amounts, gained me not only a cadre of friends but an occasional helping hand. In time, I pulled us out of homelessness and returned us to a more normal lifestyle, but the hot days of that summer will never leave me. Neither will what I learned from them.

One

After nearly six years as a housewife, I was ready for a change. My life was not terrible . . . far from it. But it lacked something—excitement perhaps—and I was determined to fill the void.

My husband Tom and I had a luxury apartment in a suburb west of Washington, D.C. The apartment itself wasn't outstanding. Just a nice little two bedroom on the bottom floor. We had a small yard and a patio, landscaped with the appropriate evergreen shrubs embedded in sparkling white gravel.

I spent my days being pregnant, playing with babies, and then toddlers; cleaning, cooking, walking, and watching a lot of TV. I was also perpetually in pursuit of fruit juice stains in the white carpets I so badly wanted when we moved in. It was a relatively boring, but necessary existence. I could barely distinguish between the days. Was it Monday or Wednesday? Did it matter? Each day, I would do the same thing. Tom would be up before the sun and head to work. I rarely saw him. I could hear him clanking around in the kitchen, maybe I heard the shower turn on, but I was never fully awake when he left. Usually my second child, Lydia—just fourteen months younger than Matthew and still nursing—would be in bed alongside me. I had long since learned that the best way to get a few extra hours sleep was just to bring the baby into bed with me.

I dragged myself out of bed around 7:00 A.M. Matthew would undoubtedly be calling me from his crib, and he and Lydia would both need changing. I pulled on sweatpants, put my hair in a ponytail, and carried them both—one on each hip—to the living room. The middle of our apartment was one large room divided only by a kitchen island and the dividing piece of trim between the living room carpet and the kitchen tile. The dining room table resided between the two. The kids' bedroom was on one side of the apartment. Tom's and mine was on the other. We had two bathrooms, a half bath by the door and a full bath in our bedroom, so this was truly luxury living. Still in a post-college mode, I had lined the walls with many books in milk crates. A futon sofa in the living room along with a couple of side tables and the television were really the only pieces of grown-up furniture in the place. Every other dime and piece of credit I had was spent on what I affectionately called Kid Stuff. Two cribs, high chairs, strollers, walkers, changing tables—you name it, I owned it. Someone should really post a warning sign that tells you all of the things you will be required to buy once you have a baby. But I didn't mind and tried to be happy in the life I had wanted so much that I left college for it.

A couple of years went by, and I was pregnant yet again.

There were times being pregnant and having children felt like the only thing I could do well. The only thing I was good for. And frankly, it was the only thing I wanted to do. Even though I constantly searched the classifieds for a job, I didn't know what I was looking for. A different life maybe. A life like the one described by the people in my ever-growing stack of adventure books: mushers, bush pilots, midwives in the backwoods. The children's naptime was my time to escape to a life much more interesting than my own. Someday, I would think, I will have adventures. Someday, we will go to Alaska, and I will finally learn to fly a plane.

I have wanted to fly since I was a child. I wanted to apply to the Naval Academy, but my mother talked me out of it—convincing me that the military was a little too regimented for someone of my, shall we say, independent spirit? I was accepted at an aeronautical university in the Southwest, but was too chicken to leave my family so far behind. I wondered a lot in that apartment—how would my life be different if I had followed that dream? Or what if I had spent the extra year working in the U.S. Senate as a page, instead of coming home early, homesick again? I would never have met Tom in that McDonald's in Vermont, just thirty minutes from my family's farm. In my soul-mate seeking giddiness, I thought that was destiny. Lately, I have come to think of it as sheer stupidity. Not that I regretted having children. Far from it. In fact, for the first time in my life, I felt as though I had a purpose. But Tom, that was another story altogether.

I met Tom in a McDonald's only a month after returning home from a semester as a U.S. Senate Page. And while I was not immediately taken with him, the way he turned and looked at me made me feel, at first, like I must have something hanging out of my nose; and second, after cleverly, coyly wiping at said nose, that he might be interested in me. I was with my little sister, Libby. We were driving back from the only mall within miles of our farm, and I was starving. While Libby ordered the works, I, now fully conscious that a decidedly cute guy might have an interest in me, ordered a Diet Coke.

He joined us. We talked, we laughed, and Libby rolled her eyes a lot. We exchanged numbers and within a week were inseparable. We *were* John and Yoko. But we had nothing in common. He was a student at the local tech school. I was a political science head in my junior year in high school. But it was great to be loved. And it was nice to have someone older to hang out with—and to brag about to my high school friends.

It was fun and romantic to be in love at sixteen. And Tom didn't disappoint. Once, for my birthday, he came to my house in his beat-up old truck, the back of which he had filled with sand. He drove me to a creek near my house and parked over it, at a spot where the creek and the path were almost level. He set out a blanket, and we sat in the back, dangling our feet off the back, drinking nonalcoholic sparkling cider.

Tom followed me to American University in Washington, D.C. But I found myself, after one semester, in the financial aid office trying to figure out how I was going to pay for my next year of school. My parents were having financial difficulties of their own and could no longer afford to supplement the costly tuition. Even with their difficulties, financial aid was determined based on the previous year's tax returns. Those being in good order, I was, as my father would say, S.O.L. (shit out of luck).

"Well, I don't make very much at the toy store and I'm living off of my income and my boyfriend's," I pleaded with the lady at the helm of financial aid.

"You can't declare yourself independent until someone else either stops claiming you as a dependent on their tax returns, or you get married," she said. "And if someone stops claiming you, you have to have been independent for at least two years."

"But if I get married?" I asked.

"Then you can be declared independent right away," she said.

"Married, huh?"

And there it is. No romantic rooftop proposals, no down on one knee, "Will you marry me?" scenes. I simply informed Tom that if I was to continue going to college, he would have to marry me. It seemed, at the time, to be the easiest way to solve the problem at hand and I was in love, so what was the big deal?

"OK," he said. "We're practically married now."

Looking back, it was the single most unselfish thing Tom ever did for me. So during the spring semester, in between classes and working at the toy store, I planned a wedding. I wanted a regular white dress, tuxedo wedding. I didn't know that for thirty dollars we could have just done it at the courthouse. I just assumed weddings required parties and white dresses. My parents, who rented out our farm in Vermont and moved to a nearby Maryland suburb of D.C., offered up their house as the wedding hall, so that cut our expenses down considerably. Through gritted teeth and disappointed sighs—the same teeth and sighs used when they first discovered a condom wrapper in my laundry—they paid for a caterer and strained their poor finances even more by buying my dress and renting chairs and all the other accoutrements I thought were required for a wedding.

We lived in a little cockroach-infested studio apartment. We had bars on the window and were in honeymoon heaven. Meanwhile, school was becoming more and more mundane. While I showed up at Japanese class at 8:00 A.M. wearing sweatpants and a T-shirt, the other students were there, ready to learn, in suits. What planet were these people from? I began to spend class time reading baby books and daydreaming about having a baby. I can see now that I suffered from some form of the grass-is-always-greener syndrome. I envied Tom his "real" job and salary. He was out there, meeting people, working in his field—doing what he loved to do and frankly, I was not getting on socially at school. The few friends I did make lived in the dorms and went to parties. Parties I either never found out about, or never went to because I felt obligated to be home for Tom who had worked all day. Between my lack of friends and with my increasing boredom in class, I just couldn't see how I was going to make it through college.

American University was, and I imagine still is, a place where professionals are made. Somewhere in my head, I guess I thought I had already done the Washington thing, and I was ready to move on to my next adventure—pregnancy. I quit school at the end of my freshman year—technically, I took a leave of absence—and pursued a full-time job in a restaurant, bartending and waiting tables and earning more money than I had ever seen before. Tom, who was indifferent to my decision to leave school ("Whatever you want to do . . ."), was all for my full-time job, which gave us more disposable income than any eighteen- and twenty-two-year-old should have. We also decided that it would be stupid to try and get pregnant, but that we wouldn't continue to exercise birth control (I was on the pill at the time), and if we got pregnant, then great and if not, that was OK too. I had read so many stories about women who couldn't get pregnant that I thought it was a relatively difficult thing to do. It turns out I'm incredibly fertile, and I think we only had to think the word *pregnant* and I was.

After becoming pregnant, I had to leave my job at the restaurant because I was stricken with the worst case of morning (noon and night) sickness ever and was useless near anything with a smell. We also left our infested apartment in Washington and found our luxury apartment in the 'burbs where I was to begin my new life as a housewife.

My parents, who had taken the whole wedding thing fairly well—except that both started smoking again—were absolutely dumbfounded when I became pregnant. I think they agreed to the marriage only because they knew I was doing it to stay in school and because I did love Tom. But a baby was almost too much. There was much more gritting of teeth and desperate sighing, but even if they wanted to disown their oldest daughter, they did nothing but help and see me through morning sickness and back pain. I even stayed at their house in the final weeks of my pregnancy and right after Matthew was born.

The strange thing is, as a teenager, I never imagined having children. At fifteen, I had feminist leanings. I would not, I decided, be enslaved by children like I thought my own mother was. My own mother was everything I didn't want to be when I grew up. She was a housewife. She lived for her children, silly woman! She ran us around to all our various activities; when we weren't around, she gardened. What a positively boring existence, my arrogant fifteen-year-old self thought.

And here I was at nineteen, married and pregnant. The once future president of the United States. It took me a long time to realize that my own mother, who had lived this life already, was the one who tried to stop me.

My friend Laura and I spent many hours walking around the neighborhood, poking fun at the families with nannies and new white sofas—the likes of which we neither desired nor could afford.

"Ah yes, the Brennans have gotten their third new car in the last two years," she would say in her snootiest voice. "I was planning myself on getting a new BMW, but don't you know that my 1979 Suburban will soon be a classic."

"Indeed," I replied. "And who knows how much my rusty, nearly floorless Subaru wagon will appreciate in the years to come—a sound investment if I do say so." And then we would laugh hysterically. Laura was one of those friends who I never had to put on a show for. If the house was covered in toys when she visited, she just stepped over them and helped me make peanut butter and jelly sandwiches for the kids.

We were not rich. In fact, Tom and I were not even closing in on financially comfortable and had all too easily gotten ourselves bogged down in credit card debt. But I could relate my distasteful conversations with credit card collection officers to Laura without feeling embarrassed.

I worried constantly about money and was always dodging the phone because one credit card company or another was forever calling and threatening me. Laura calmed me down and made me realize that there wasn't a lot they could do. If I just made the effort to pay them, she said, no matter what the amount, they would leave me alone and work with me.

Tom was ever cool about financial matters—certain, I think, that the money would fall from the sky, or my parents. He also had a knack for wrecking cars, putting our insurance through the roof and for taking money out of the ATM thinking, *If it says I have money, then I must have it*—and then letting me bounce checks all over town. He constantly told me, "There are no debtors' prisons anymore." This was his way of telling me not to nag him about collections calls.

I thus threw myself into an unorthodox education, driven by a desire to supplement our meager income and be somebody. I could not accept that I was ordinary. Between this and what I am convinced now was a constant state of postpartum depression, I continually searched for something that would help me rise above my ordinary life. Being a mother by choice at nineteen was extraordinary to me, but when that mother turns twenty-one or twenty-three, she becomes less interesting and more, well, normal.

I started a babysitting service and was able to contribute some to our income while I read a multitude of books on how to start businesses or biographies of people who had done amazing things. One week it was a musher who had won the Iditarod, the next it was a PTA mom who had run for governor.

Despite the excitement Tom instilled in our lives with his absentminded driving, it was a calm—if not affluent—life, to say the least. And while I can't say that it was all I had hoped my world would be, it seemed necessary at the time. My dreams were just that—dreams. I didn't want to send my kids to day care and I really didn't know what I wanted to be when I grew up anyway. Being Mom seemed to be just as good a job as any.

Tom, however, was visibly unhappy and had been making plans of his own—not late night, sit up with your wife and talk plans, but real plans that would change our lives forever.

Two

For the first years of our married life, Tom dragged himself home every day from his job as a computer technician and lay down on the couch with a ragged copy of *Walden* or *Backwoods Home* magazine. I can't say that the idea of living a more simplified life didn't appeal to me . . . but in truth, my life was already pretty simple. Besides, Laura Ingalls had already influenced my life. I already baked bread and cookies. I learned how to sew. I read my books about Alaska. I tried to make apple jelly from the apples I bought at the farmers' market—I failed miserably, but I tried. I pictured myself cooking on the woodstove Tom raved about while the children played peacefully on the floor. The thing of it was that I was already living that simple life—except that my stove was electric, and the children rarely played peacefully.

I thought that maybe one day we would save for a rustic little cabin to escape to on vacations—and then come back to our real life. I pictured myself eventually becoming the PTA president when the kids finally went off to school. I saw myself as the ultimate volunteer mom: Cub Scout leader, Girl Scout leader, library helper, and cookie-baker. I would do it all. I had just finished reading the biography of Madeline Kunin, the former governor of Vermont. I read about her being a mom and working for the kids; then finding her way into city politics and eventually running for governor. I imagined doing the same. My desire to be more, to do more was never satiated. I just had to settle for not doing more right now.

Tom had a different image altogether. Noisy neighbors did more than bother him, they enraged him. He was tired of commuting, tired of driving—tired of the proverbial rat race, and I guess that in his place I might feel the same, so I tried to be nothing but supportive. I had no idea how difficult that would be.

Tom came home from work one day with an unfamiliar gleam in his eye. He loosened his tie and told me that he quit his job.

"Really?" I said, trying to remain calm. Being a bitchy wife is generally the last thing that one wants to be accused of at a time like this. "That's a little sudden. Did something in particular happen?"

"No, I've just decided we need to live more simply. There is no need for all of this," he said, waving his arms around the room, ostensibly pointing out all of the material things we had accumulated over the years.

"If we didn't have a need or desire for all of these things, Michelle, I wouldn't need to work so hard at a job I hate to keep them."

"Well, is it your job you hate or the things? I mean, if you had a job you liked, would the stuff we have to pay for matter?" I asked. I was beginning to feel more than a little insulted. I had worked hard to make life pleasant in our tiny home.

"But where does it all go?" he said accusingly. "I work and work and work, and it all seems to get thrown away—on nothing."

"All right—now just calm the hell down before you get too nasty," I said. "Do you need a detailed list of all of our expenses? You know how fast money goes."

This was a little too much. I didn't spend a lot of money on myself; I only owned one pair of sneakers and a pair of loafers.

In fact, I suffered from an enormous case of what I call *motherguilt*. It's that Ma Walton in all mothers, I think. The part of mothers that said *My new coat equals four new pairs of shoes for the children*, or swimming lessons or whatever. It is simply not possible for me to look through a rack of clothing without bringing along a rack of guilt. Ma Ingalls gave up winter coats and a new cookstove so her children could have a shiny new tin cup at Christmas; the least I can do is give up a new pair of jeans so my kids can learn to swim.

But these explanations were wearing thin on Tom. He slumped his shoulders and shifted his weight, irritated with my obvious inability to understand basic truths.

"You are not understanding what I am saying," he said. "I'm not saying that you're a bad person for wanting these things. I'm saying that society is making you want these things, and if we got away from this society, then you would no longer have the desire to watch TV and buy the crap that's advertised on it."

"Tom, I'm not some child who sees an Easy Bake Oven on TV and needs to have it right now," I said. "What are you saying that we have to have? Like food? How about car insurance? I'll grant you that the cable TV is a luxury, but it's not like we go out anymore and have any fun, so I will keep that luxury as the only adult voices I get to hear during the day, thank you very much."

I wanted to go on. Several cheap shots crossed my mind—like his car wrecks—but I shut my mouth.

And even though he began talking slowly, as if to a stupid child who couldn't comprehend even the most basic of philosophies, I still held my tongue. I wanted to say: "Well, at least I know how to drive!" or better still, "Fuck you!" Not such intelligent comebacks, I know, and I didn't say them. I didn't say anything. I felt defensive, and I felt small. I couldn't do anything. I was pregnant (again) with two young children. What would I do with myself? Nothing, that's what. So I sat and listened to him berate me and "my lifestyle"—which he failed to mention was also his lifestyle—and wondered how I could have been so stupid to think that this is what life is all about. Trained for nothing, I could do nothing to support us.

"No, but they sell you an image." He was still ranting. "You see a perfect little suburban sitcom family, and you want that. You want a perfect house and a new car and for the kids to be dressed for Sunday dinner all of the time."

"I don't think that's true," I replied. "You're not being fair—you've been just as much a part of choosing this life as I have. Don't try and make it sound like I've trapped you. If anyone is trapped, it's me for godsakes—I'm the one who is here all day long, with no one to talk to and nothing to do but clean up after you!"

But was it true? Was I in danger of repeating the same life my mother had lived when I was a child? Was I destined to watch soap operas all day and bake cookies for the PTA? That couldn't be true, could it?

"I'm going for a walk," he said haughtily. "Think about what I said."

"Think about what I said," I mimicked like a child as he walked down the porch steps. I slammed the door after him.

The slamming of the door woke up Lydia. I heard crying from the kids' bedroom and tried to run toward it, but my seven months' pregnant belly prohibited me from going too quickly. Pulling myself along, waddling against the still air of the room, I felt like a pathetic mountain climber, sans mountain, unprepared for the journey of just a few feet.

Lydia was upset from the yelling she heard, but was quickly soothed back to sleep. Matthew, just over a year older than Lydia, was rarely awakened by anything. You could run screaming fire trucks through his room, and he would still sleep. When he was a baby I thought he was deaf because he rarely responded to noises. It turns out he was just ignoring me— even as a baby. He still ignores me when I call him, but he's the first to know almost everything in the house. He knew the moment his father was home from work just by the sound of the car door on the street. Though we heard car doors close all day long—our parking lot was fairly busy—Matthew knew which one was his dad's, whether it was 5:00 P.M. or 8:00 P.M.

I took a long bath. I lay there in the tub, watching my now huge belly move like a wiggly Jell-O mold with the fits and starts of the baby beneath. I laughed as a kick would poke out, and then I would poke it back. This kid loved to move around. Just when I thought a foot was poking me, a big wash of movement would overwhelm me, and I could swear that I saw a butt go by.

Tom walked into the bathroom.

"I heard you laughing," he said.

"I am assuming you have some sort of plan, otherwise you wouldn't have quit your job," I said as pleasantly as possible. "Why don't you just tell me what it is and then we can sort it out."

"Well, a guy at work . . ."

"What guy?"

"Bill, OK? Bill has a cabin in Maine, and he said that he has a neighbor that is selling his cabin. It's supposed to be really great. A little rough, but not uninhabitable. Bill is planning on going up there this weekend to scope out carpentry work, and he wants me to go along."

"This weekend? I can't go this weekend? What about the baby?"

"No, no. Of course you can't, but I could. I could go up and check it out and be back in a few days."

"Uh huh."

"I could take pictures and bring them back to show you the cabin."

"Uh huh."

"Is that all you're going to say?"

"What do you want me to say, Tom? It's obviously what you want to do, so go do it. Far be it from me to stand in the way of another person's dream. Just try not to forget about us back here."

We went to bed that night in silence. But that was nothing new. Intimacy and intensity had long since left our relationship. We were more like good friends who had sex occasionally. Very occasionally. I just happened to get pregnant almost every time. I thought about going back on the pill between pregnancies, but I was usually still nursing a baby when I became pregnant with the next, and I'm actually allergic to condoms. Besides, I loved having babies. I loved being pregnant, and I had "planned" each baby. Perhaps planned is too strong a word. It was more like I would think one day: Wouldn't it be nice to have another one? And then before I had thought it all the way through, I was already pregnant again. But Tom had a decent job with advancement potential, and I was trying to clear up our credit. I was learning how to be frugal and accepting of the fact that I couldn't live like my parents on less than half the budget. We had even started looking at townhouses in the area. I thought I had it all figured out.

But the friendship between us was waning. Every conversation was tinged with guilt and admonition tossed in one direction or the other. I can't say that I have ever been an easy person to please, and I know my harebrained schemes must have been annoying, like the time I was going to become the next Lillian Vernon and start a catalog business from home. And I did spend too much money on stuff for the kids sometimes and then complain that we didn't have enough, but I just wanted them to have everything I had as a child. Of course, I was spoiled rotten as far as stuff was concerned. I was an only child for a long time before my two younger sisters came along. My father told me once that he and my mother used to tell people in line at Toys 'R Us that they had nine children at Christmas because they had gotten me so many things.

I tried hard to remember what I loved so much about Tom, what made me practically hijack him and force him to come to D.C. with me in the first place. Tom was so grown up when I met him, but he had a sad, sensitive side too. He was adopted by his parents when he was almost two. The story he tells, the one that made me cry almost every time, was that his mother wanted to send him back to the convent because he was an ugly baby, but his father said he looked like he would be a good worker, so they kept him. At sixteen, I heard this story and wanted to love and care for this person who had been treated so poorly. He had grown up without knowing what it was like to be a part of a loving family and I wanted to give him that, more than anything. Something took over in me when I was sixteen, a maternal side I didn't know I had.

Maybe a simple life would be better. Maybe I would learn something. Even so, I wasn't enthused about the massive change; the idea of moving two kids and a baby was tiring just to think about. I considered divorcing him and staying in my house. But I knew that I couldn't manage alone without his income.

Laura once asked me why I didn't just divorce him if he bugged me so much and I said—I remember this distinctly—that I didn't see how my life would be any different if I divorced him. I would still need his money, and I would still be home with kids all the time. The only difference would be that I would never get to have sex, as opposed to the once every three months that I currently got to have it. Laura thought I was kidding.

He left the next day. There wasn't a lot to say. I wished him luck and told him to call me when he got to a phone. It wasn't like he had never gone away before. He frequently left us behind for one business trip or another. He always took the "good" car—the company car that I was never allowed to drive. I was left with my old, rusting Subaru wagon that I didn't trust to get me to the mailbox, much less the store, so I usually stayed home.

I was trying to get excited by this plan to go live in a cabin in the woods. Inspired by National Geographic videos of

Alaska and far too many *Northern Exposure* reruns, I lost myself in the planning. Tom's magazines about the "good life" living off the grid still came to the house weekly, and so I tried to get excited about a life of growing vegetables and chopping wood. I really wanted this to make things better. If our relationship was suffering because Tom was unhappy in his work, then who was I to say no? Didn't I take him for better or worse? This certainly had to be better. He would be happy; therefore we would be happy. People did it all of the time. They left jobs and went to find their bliss in a new place. I was always watching these people on TV or reading about them in the very books I coveted. They left the rat race and sought out new, fulfilling lives. Maybe we wouldn't have a lot of money, but we didn't now, so what would change?

I'll admit to not being pleased about the news that I was pregnant again.

"Haven't you two figured out what causes this yet?" was my father's response. Since I first became pregnant with Matthew, telling my father about my impending pregnancies was more like informing him that a family member had died. Each time was like a little stab in his heart—another disappointment from his once-promising oldest daughter. This time around, I could finally see it from his side, but it certainly wasn't anything I couldn't handle. As the months wore on, I got more and more excited for the birth. It was natural for me, I couldn't help but be excited about it.

Tom was gone for almost two months, sending money home every month from work he found as a logger. I was already quite good at the art of self-sufficiency. I always bought flour and oats in bulk, so that I could get through the times when Tom was away at conventions or off helping some client in another city. He was usually dependable, but sometimes he would be gone for a week or more and would forget to have his company mail me his paycheck. He was always sorry, but he didn't seem to understand how difficult it was for me to be alone in the house all the time with two little ones and another on the way. According to him, I was always the "lucky one" because I got to stay home and "do nothing" all day, while he went out and worked hard to support us.

But this time, Tom was gone for more than a few days. His job logging or doing construction or whatever it was paid $10 an hour—leaving him little to send home. And we were left back in the suburbs with $5 in cash and a dwindling supply of food. I received his last paycheck from the business machines company in the mail. That helped me pay the bills, and then I cashed in his 401K, which wasn't much, but it paid the rent for a couple of months. I had been babysitting, but had stopped months before, right before I found out I was pregnant again. In what I was later to determine was a hormonal fit, I had canceled my services to my two regular customers because they never paid me on time. I was sick of having to ask for money all the time and one Friday night, before leaving for a weekend at my parents' house, I left angry phone messages telling them to stop dropping their children off if they weren't going to pay me. The stick turned pink over that weekend. As it was, I couldn't have handled sitting for more children than my own during the first five months of my pregnancy anyway. I usually spend the first four or five months either lying on the couch moaning or expressing my all-day-long morning sickness in the bathroom.

It was getting bad at home, though, and I was regretting having made enemies out of my former babysitting clients. I was down to oatmeal for breakfast and lunch and apples and my homemade bread for dinner. I altered the bread with the assortment of spices and herbs I had, but I couldn't make much of a meal out of dill weed, cinnamon, and celery seed. Tom called to say that he had sent money to us three days before, but I had yet to see it. I was enraged not only by this apparent lack of concern for our well-being but also at my own inability to come up with an income.

I sat on the porch one morning, watching the children play in the backyard and wondering how on earth we could look so normal and yet be so askew. I literally could not find two nickels to rub together aside from the five-dollar bill that was in the music box on my nightstand. Fortunately, Tom's insurance lasted us through the end of this pregnancy. I was crazy from the anxiety and to make me even crazier, the baby had become a gymnast, keeping me awake at night. And when the baby wasn't tumbling, the Braxton-Hicks contractions—the sometimes painful fake preparatory contractions of late pregnancy—were killing me. They were constant, but my midwife said it was just normal in a person who had already had a couple of kids, especially when they were so close together.

There had to be something I could do. I went to college, even if I didn't finish and even if I *was* an English major. But there weren't a lot of options. I had to laugh when I heard a guy on public radio a few days before sheepishly admit to having been an English major, after saying how he loved his job in sales. Either way, at least I was intelligent once upon a time; there had to be something I could do to make some money. I flipped with a certain franticness through the weekly newspaper that came free to our door and searched for something—anything—that would give me enough money to put gas in the car and go to the grocery store. I didn't mention any of it to my parents. They were having their doubts about Tom already and I couldn't handle their disapproval.

There were plenty of ads looking for people to stuff envelopes and assemble products from home. I had decided to apply for a babysitting job when a notice caught my attention. It was for the weekly farmers' market in Baltimore. They weren't advertising for vendors, but I thought I would call anyway and see if they could use anyone who sold bread. Laura was always telling me how my bread was better than anything she could get in the store.

The woman who answered the phone sounded as though she had just gotten off a crab boat. The smell of fish was practically detectable through the phone. I could barely make out her description of the market, but when she told me to "Come on down and show us what you got," I knew I was in business.

I spent all night baking every type of bread combination that I could think up with my limited supplies. I made cinnamon bread, oatmeal bread, Italian bread, dinner rolls, foccacia, and braided herb bread. I was determined to look as professional as possible. I had a supply of brown paper lunch bags in the pantry, remnants of a grocery store trip ages ago, and proceeded to write my bakery name: MICHELLE'S BAKED GOODS in very flowery handwriting, along with my "business" phone number and address.

I tossed and turned on the couch for about an hour, my stomach aching with anxiety and my back aching from the weight of my belly. Bright and early at 5:00 A.M., I loaded all the bread into the car and said a little prayer that there would be enough gas to coast us into the gas station in town. The air was crisp and cold, and the sky was not yet light. I had filled milk crates with my bread and covered them with different swatches of fabrics and blankets that I found throughout the house, to make it look like I knew what I was doing. I stumbled along the path with the heavy milk crates filled to overflowing with my hopes for a new beginning.

Then I went back into the house and dressed my two sleepy children, gave them each a piece of bread that wasn't suitable for selling, aesthetically speaking, and tucked them into the car under several woolly blankets. The car sputtered, gasping for a gassy breath as I coaxed it into the station. I pumped in my last five dollars, and remembered with a start that I didn't have change for any customers I might have. Oh well, I thought, they'll just have to have correct change.

I knew where the market was held from having been a customer there myself several times, but being a part of it was a different experience altogether. Cammie, the daughter of the woman I had spoken to on the phone, met the children and me at the parking lot entrance and showed us to our space.

"Oh, I don't know if I'm supposed to have a space," I said. "The lady on the phone said I'd have to show her my breads first."

"Don't you worry, I can tell right now that you'll do just fine," she said. It seemed a little silly to feel so proud of something as simple as bread, but I was a little punchy from staying up so late, and I was counting on this market to provide enough money for some food and enough gas to get back home, so I went with it.

It was interesting to sit in our lawn chairs and watch the people walk by our makeshift booth. The market officially opened at 7:00 A.M., and we sold five loaves of bread at $3 each almost immediately. I had enough to pay the $10 fee for the booth—Cammie said she would make me last on her route around the market—and to buy juice for Matthew and Lydia.

My nerves were starting to settle a bit, but my stomach was still on edge. To pass the time between customers, we picked out people in the crowds and tried to guess what they did for a living. Matthew guessed that every man was a fireman and every woman a doctor. Lydia was a little more creative: A woman in a long dress was a dancer and a man in a suit was a movie star.

At the end of the morning, we had $180 to take home. $180. Enough to put gas in the car and buy food and enough ingredients to come back the next week. It wasn't a glamorous business, but it was a business, and I could do it on my own. Cammie came around and told me to bring more next time, because if people saw my larger selection they would want to buy more. I still had two loaves of bread left, which I dropped off at a friend's house on the way home. We wanted fruit salad—not bread—for lunch and we were going to have it.

When we got home, Tom and his money were there waiting. He was angry because I hadn't left him a note. As if I knew he was going to be home! He hadn't been home in three weeks. I put the kids down for a nap—they ate their lunch in the car on the way home—and sank into a chair on the porch.

"Why are you so tired?" Tom asked. I couldn't even speak. He had been gone for two months. I wanted to throttle him, and I wanted to cry all at the same time. I fell asleep instead.

Three

I had Alex at home on a stormy March night, and Tom returned north shortly after. I bided my time with bread baking and breastfeeding my newborn. When he turned a month old, and with no reason to stall any longer, we headed up north. Very north. The far north of Maine. A place where the majority of accepted currency is Canadian. This would be the first time in almost four months that we would all live together full-time again. Tom had to work and couldn't come down to help, so I was left to travel the road from Maryland to Maine on my own. My parents helped me pack most of our things and stored them in their garage for me back in Vermont. They also tried their best to talk me out of moving to a cabin in the woods, but I was just as hardheaded as I had ever been. I was destined for adventure and ready to try something new.

To most people, traveling with two preschoolers and an infant would be a nightmare, but to me, it was merely horrendous. The trip between Maryland and northern Maine took us two days. It would probably take a normal traveler less, but if you have to stop every forty-five minutes for a bathroom or to let the kids stretch their legs or to nurse the baby, you don't get very far very fast.

I swore that I would never insult my rusty old Subaru again if it got us where we were going safely. Whoever it was I swore to answered back with a driving snowstorm during the homestretch—or what my *Maine Atlas and Gazetteer* called the homestretch. It was actually a 250-mile flat highway that stretched on forever. I had no idea that it was so flat anywhere in New England. At this point, I was so used to the mountains and winding roads that made Lydia throw up, that the flatness was almost a cause for celebration.

But after about thirty miles, driving the flat road became nothing but sheer boredom. It was pine tree after pine tree, broken up only by the occasional moose sighting.

Mount Katahdin—northern Maine's only claim to fame as far as I knew—is a welcome sight to flat-weary drivers. It stands straight up in the middle of what appears to be a scrubby northern desert. On my frequent travels over the next couple of years between my parent's Vermont home and the cabin, Katahdin became my one landmark—my gateway to the rest of the world.

The April snow, an infrequent site in Maryland, fell heavier and heavier. I spent the last money I earned at the farmers' market on new, studded snow tires, so while I couldn't go as quickly as the Jeep Cherokees and Ford Explorers that were leaving me in their wake, I was able to plod steadily on.

The image of a sweet little cabin nestled in the snow with a roaring fire kept me going when the sky fell dark and the snow began to have that *Star Wars* effect on my windshield. Like I was going at warp speed through space, the stars coming at me ten, twenty, one hundred at a time. Sometimes they formed a tunnel and I could see past them, but other times it was as if they were plastered to the windshield. My head ached from concentrating on them. I felt like I was going too fast, but a glimpse at my speedometer showed I was going only 30 mph in a 65 mph zone.

A gas station sign shone like a beacon through the trees—I assumed they were trees—since I couldn't actually see them off the highway. And I followed the exits and the turns presented to me until I reached it. Civilization. After driving in such quiet for so long—the kids had long since fallen asleep—it felt so reassuring to pull into the snow-covered driveway of the station, brilliantly lit in an otherwise black night. I parked at the pump closest to the store and sat there for a moment, letting my eyes rest, and basking in the glow of the neon beer signs hanging on the walls.

A glance at the map, a squeeze of gas in the tank, and a fresh cup of coffee to fortify my journey, and we were off again. The kids actually remained asleep through the whole stop. Of course as soon as I was steadily on the road again, the baby started to stir, so I was pleased to see that we were finally approaching our exit. It turned out we were really only a short drive from Belton, an actual city, when the snow cleared. Belton is more like a small town with a city for a title, but it did sport a grocery store, a Wal-Mart, and a variety of other necessities.

Listening to a baby squirm in his car seat is alternately painful and quite humorous. Alex wrinkled up his nose and moved his little arms like a boxer trying to punch his way out of sleep, and then with a good kick, he would fitfully fall back into his slumber. His car seat was in the passenger seat, so I could watch him, and Matthew and Lydia could fight each other in peace. He looked just like me when I woke up in the morning, trying desperately to fight it off, but somehow the waking world just kept coming.

I gave him my knuckle to suck on to keep him busy and to keep him from screaming out for a boob, but I knew it wouldn't last long. The snow had let up a little, but I still had to find my way in the dark to this new place. I tacked the directions onto the dashboard with a staple I found on the floor and tried to read them, follow the few street signs I could find, and keep Alex quiet all at the same time. A turn here and there led to a long, bumpy—obviously unpaved—road that had yet to be plowed. Fortunately a larger vehicle than my own had carved its way through the road, and I was able to follow in its tracks.

"Come on, baby," I said, softly trying to coax my poor Subaru along the trail. I saw what appeared to be house lights in the distance and was hoping that this was the cabin. I paid so much attention to the house lights that I didn't notice that my headlights were slowly dimming. At one point they went completely out. I stopped the car, but kept it running in fear of not being able to get it going again and pushed open my door. It was quite a heave, too, because the heavy snow we had traveled through earlier on the highway had piled up to about a foot and a half on this road, and I had to push through it to open the door. I was wearing my sneakers for traveling, so the first step into the knee-high snow was a treat. I hopped through it to the front of the car and realized that the front of my poor car had become a virtual snowplow. There was a V-shaped formation of snow completely blocking my headlights and pushing a path for the rest of the car.

I kicked the snow away with a great hopping motion that kept my feet and legs out of the pile while simultaneously clearing the car. The kids, awake now, laughed at my funny show—now in the spotlight because the lights were free to illuminate it—and I hopped back through the snow and dove into the car. My jeans and socks were packed with wet snow, but I ignored it knowing that I would be warm soon enough. I took off my shoes, emptied them out, and carefully put the car into gear and crept along the path.

If there hadn't been a path, and if I hadn't known that the best way to get a car to move in snow is to go slow—not to step on it—then I might have been stuck there. But my brain was fortunately back on, and I released the clutch slowly and drove the car in first gear all the way down the road. I was feeling quite proud of myself for being able to drive in such a professional manner.

I passed the house with the lights when I saw Tom's truck in the next driveway over. A faint light, emanating from what I later determined was a kerosene lamp, was in the small front window. Pulling up to the cabin after our slow crawl through the snow, I felt my stomach drop to my knees. Alex had the exact same reaction I would have had if I were an infant. He began to scream at the top of his lungs.

Tom came running out—excited to show us all of his "improvements."

"Here you go guys," he said to Matt and Lydia as he picked them up and carried them through the snow to the door. I picked up Alex and held him in the front seat of the car while I slipped my sneakers back on.

"And this is the kitchen," he said, standing in the room with the wood cookstove, a small gas cookstove, and a table. From what I could tell, the whole house was the kitchen. There was a sink in the corner, but no faucet—no water. There was a little stove that appeared to run on propane. There was also a small pot-bellied woodstove near the front door.

"Where's the refrigerator, Daddy?" Lydia asked, now wide awake.

"We don't need a refrigerator," Tom said proudly. "In the winter we can keep our things in that cooler outside, and in the summer we can keep them in the spring house."

"What's a spring house?" Matthew asked.

"A spring house is a little house built around the well where the water comes from," Tom replied.

"Where's my bed?" Matthew asked.

"You'll have to share with Lydia over there in that corner," Tom said, not the slightest bit concerned that the children had just moved from a place where there was carpet on the floor— and, well, walls—to a place where every board was exposed, and there was no insulation, much less anything to cover the floor.

Their questions were endless, but I was speechless.

My husband has lost his mind, I thought. Ever cheerful, though, I unloaded the kids and our things, and we began our adventure.

The cabin was dark. There were no separate rooms. It was one big room with corners designated for the various events of life. There was a table with some mismatched chairs on the other side of the door. The dining room, I presumed.

That first night, the children and I bundled up together on the floor, on top of and under blankets. I lay there, awake, between my sleeping children, wondering what on earth I had gotten myself into. I couldn't believe, then, that the thin uninsulated walls could possibly keep us warm. The wind, which gathered speed across the treeless flats that made up our "front yard," whistled violently through every crack and crevice.

Tom, of course, was unfazed by the sound—he was used to it I supposed—as he slept on a couch made up of cushions from the inside of an RV. Upon closer inspection in the morning, it appeared that the majority of items in the cabin were from someone's old RV. The windows were small and cranked out and up; the small gas cookstove, even the screen door in the back, had all come from a Winnebago—the logo was everywhere. I could only imagine the state of the poor vehicle in order to be reincarnated in this way.

"Isn't it great?" Tom asked. "They reused everything."

"Hmmm . . ." was my only reply. I was answering Tom like that a lot lately. And it wasn't that I wished to be snobbish, but one had to wonder: What exactly made this Tom's manifestation of paradise?

Before we left civilization behind, my mother stayed for a few days to help me pack. My mother wasn't exactly into being a grandmother. I'm not sure if it was the fact that I made her a grandmother so young, or that she didn't want to deal with crying babies, but let's just say that while she loved it when we came for a visit, she wasn't offering to do a lot of babysitting. And that was OK. I accepted that well enough. I liked staying home, and let's face it, I didn't exactly have an active adult social calendar.

But during her stay, I could tell she knew I was making a huge mistake. I wouldn't have admitted to it in a million years then, and she didn't say it out loud—although she had earned the right. During those years after I left college, my father always made his disappointment known, but my mother had never said a word. She had always run interference between me and my father before—and after—I would tell them I was pregnant again, and she always tried to be happy for me. "As long as you're happy," was her most common refrain. And the envelope she handed me said it all. I wasn't sure whether or not to be insulted, but I was certainly grateful. I was shocked and almost handed it back, but couldn't. I've never known how to show gratitude properly. I've gotten better about this as I've grown older, but part of me just has such guilt when someone gives me something. I think my silent reaction, which is really just surprise, comes across as smugness.

Something in me must have known I would need it. It was quite a bit actually, nearly $2,000, and for the first time, I lied to Tom and didn't tell him. When he left for his logging job on our first morning, I let him believe that I only had $150 with me—what was left of the money I had earned at my last farmer's market right before Alex was born.

I am not exactly sure why I didn't tell him that my mother had given me $2,000. It was very unlike me at the time. I was always the "all for one and one for all" kind of girl. But looking back, I know that I was learning that I couldn't trust him. I couldn't trust him to bring his money home, to support us, or even just to come home for that matter.

Tom went "logging" for a week at a time, and generally brought home a couple of hundred dollars. I have a feeling that there were men making much more, and I am not sure to this day what Tom was actually doing or what he was spending his money on during that time, but it mattered little. Our bills were few. If there had been rent on the place, I wouldn't have paid it—it wasn't worth it, and no one in his or her right mind could fathom charging for it. We had a bill for propane gas for the cookstove and even though we didn't have electricity, I did have a phone installed. The highest expense we had besides food was laundry.

On occasion I would hand wash a few much-needed items, but usually, once a week, I took on the herculean task of going to the Laundromat. For years, my least favorite day of the week was Laundromat day. It seemed that no matter where I moved to, I was destined to live in a house without a washer and dryer.

Over the years, with one, two, and then three children, the task of going to the Laundromat became less a joyful outing and more an expedition of Antarctic proportions. Loading that many clothes into the car in an assortment of containers from an army duffle bag to a large Rubbermaid tub, made the back of the car sink. You'd think I had put cement blocks in the back of the car, not something benign like a week's worth of five people's laundry!

On that first day, I piled the kids into the car with the desire of purchasing some things to make the cabin a little more livable. I headed straight for the bank and opened an account in my own name.

I must admit that although I felt good and not just a little rebellious by the action, I was also a little embarrassed when the woman who opened my account asked me if I was married.

"Yes" was my timid reply.

"So, this is a joint account?"

"No."

"Oh." She smiled a bit.

"Is that terrible?"

"It happens more often than you might think."

We went straight from the bank to the local camping/adventurers/feed and seed store. It is a common misconception that living in the wilderness requires very little. In fact, I learned rather quickly that while you might aim for complete self-sufficiency, you have to buy a lot of stuff first.

Not to mention the fact that we were woefully underprepared for winter having lived in Maryland (and with central heat). But I was not a stranger to winter. I had grown up in Vermont and knew what we needed. I bought snowsuits, new hats and mittens, and heavy-duty Arctic-worthy boots for me and the kids. Even little Alex got a snowsuit worthy of an expedition to the North Pole. I also got two down comforters, a solar shower and two futon mattresses for us to sleep on. I didn't spend all the money my mother gave us that day, but a good portion of it was gone—and I actually convinced Tom that I had purchased it all at a local Salvation Army Thrift Store. My penchant for deception was a little frightening, but so too was his total lack of knowledge about how much things actually cost.

Four

While waking up in the morning to the freezing room was a brutal endeavor, I rather enjoyed the meditative task of taking logs off the pile each morning and splitting them into small pieces that would get the stove roaring once again. My sense of pride was reinforced each morning as I awakened a few red coals from beneath the ashes and coaxed them back to life with the right amount of newspaper and small birch twigs.

By the time the kids were awakened by the constant opening and closing of the woodstove door, the room was warm, and there was hot water for an oatmeal breakfast. As the pile that Tom left us dwindled much quicker than I thought possible, I realized that I would have to find wood to burn. Bundled in our warmest gear, with Lydia and Matthew trudging through the deep snow and little Alex strapped in a red plastic sled, we went to the woods to find, well, wood.

Of course it hadn't occurred to me before heading out that

I would need the sled for the wood, and so Alex would need alternate transportation on the way back.

With an axe in one hand and the rope to Alex's sled in the other, we braved the blowing snow. On the lookout for wood that was already dead and thus dry and ready to burn, we passed several trees that would make perfectly good candidates for the year's Christmas tree. I had given Matthew and Lydia each a canvas bag to load up with sticks while we walked.

I felt almost at home trudging around in the snow, braving the elements with my children, looking for our heat. This was our adventure, I decided. And ready or not, I was going to take it on full force.

Nothing could have prepared us for homelessness better than a year without the amenities that most people in the modern age take for granted. Bathing became a ritual straight out of *Little House on the Prairie*. A large washtub in the kitchen area was filled with snow and then as it melted, water from the kettle was added. Eventually, a reasonably pleasant bathing experience could be had by anyone under four feet tall. Anyone taller than that was relegated to a solar shower.

A solar shower is a black plastic contraption sold in camping supply stores so that people not used to roughing it can have something resembling a regular morning shower while out in the woods. The idea of the black plastic is that you fill it with your cool mountain spring water and then the sun heats it up through the day. Then you spray yourself down with the hose attached to the bottom of the plastic. My version of the solar shower, particularly in winter, did not require me to shower outside. I simply strung the shower up in the kitchen in front of the woodstove and filled it half with boiling kettle water and half with melted snow. I stood in the kids' washtub and showered quickly.

And that was how we spent each day. Tom would get up early and go to whatever carpentry or logging job he found and I would make fires, bathe children, cook, clean, and do whatever else I needed to do. Without electricity, we spent a lot of time at the library. I had begun devouring the Irish section: travel books, journals, history, whatever. I spent many afternoons listening to wind whip by the windows, lying on my bed while the children played on the floor, reading about Ireland. To be honest, it wasn't a lot different than the life I had in the suburbs—except that everything was just more work.

Just doing the dishes required more energy than I usually got during my morning workouts at our old house. Hauling water, chopping the wood to heat it on the stove, and then actually doing the dishes, I probably burned more calories than I ever did on our cast-off treadmill. But while Tom was having the time of his life, the children and I were floundering in boredom. There was never enough money to go anywhere and do anything and really—unless we traveled south—there really wasn't much to do.

There was something missing in this life, I decided. Something primal and native. For so long I had wanted a dog team. There was an image of Alaska in my head, and I was yearning for adventure in my heart. Since college I had been a boring housewife, and I wanted more. The simple life wasn't quite cutting it.

So, now fully inspired by Libby Riddles' account of winning the Iditarod in *Race Across Alaska*, with children in tow and a rusty hand-me-down pickup truck, I began to collect husky dogs. I also spent the rest of my money on dog gear. I bought every book I could find on the art of mushing. I realize now that it was a frivolous and selfish thing to do, especially with children so young. But I longed not only to be adventurous but to be unique. I truly loved having the dogs around. I loved everything about them—their smell, their enthusiasm, the way they howled for me in the morning and were excited to see me. We became a team—a family—the dogs and I.

And in much the same way that I taught myself how to drive a stick shift, so did I teach myself how to mush a team of dogs. In northern Maine, if you tell even your next-door neighbor that you're going to start collecting huskies for a dogsled team, people will start dropping off dogs for you. In less than a month I became the local husky rescue operation. I had retired, sprint sled dogs, puppies, and old dogs people swore could pull. And I took them all. There was no dog I could refuse. If a dog was good at heart, then I would build it a house. People in Belton started calling me the Dog Lady. And when they asked me what I was going to do with all of them, I proclaimed to be training for the Iditarod.

My parents of course, thought I was insane. And I can't blame them. My father always believed, and still does, that you just get up and go to work every day and if you hate the job, that's OK. In fact, I think he believes you are supposed to hate your job. But, "work is just work, Shell," he'd always say. "If it was fun, they'd call it fun, but it's not, it's work."

I absolutely defied that logic. I believed, and still do, that you can love what you do and make a living at it. And I loved running dogs. As summer turned to winter, the most beautiful sight in the world for me was watching six or eight dogs running, in almost complete harmony, in front of my dogsled. Their backs glistened with snow that had fallen and formed a glaze over their outer hairs. Their collars jingled against their necklines. I felt like the Inuit version of Santa Claus. And the kids loved it too. I would take them out with me, strapping Alex in his car seat and attaching it by a bungee cord to the stanchions of the sled.

We went everywhere by dogsled—including the store. And I loved the way we turned heads. I loved the way people thought we were either cool or insane—I was never sure which. And Tom started to enjoy the dogs too. We would howl with them at night after dinner. The kids and I would sit on their doghouses, and we would start howling. It was our own night song. Every morning they woke me up with the same howl, but it was definitely better than a rooster.

I spent the year we lived in northern Maine raising dogs. Tom couldn't find work and, after the money my mother gave us evaporated into car parts, phone bills, and dog accessories, I took a job as a bartender at a local club. Tom stayed home with the kids and the dogs. It made me nervous. Tom was not the most responsible, but there was nothing I could do—we needed the money and frankly, I enjoyed going out and working. I liked seeing other people and being away from the kids for a while. It wasn't that he didn't try, but I would always come home from work early in the morning to find one of the stove burners on or the woodstove door left open. It drove me crazy.

One evening in early April, I got a call at work. I never got calls at work. Tom never called me, and I hardly knew anyone else in town. Even after almost a year, my life was restricted to the guys in the bar, the cabin, and the people I knew through dogsledding.

"Mrs. Shepherd?"

"Yes?"

"First, you need to know that your daughter is OK," the anonymous voice said.

"Who is this?" What kind of joke was this?

"Your daughter's been in an accident." We only had one car, and I had it for the evening.

"What kind of accident?"

"She's been bitten by one of your dogs."

"What? Where?" It was impossible to believe.

"On the head, on the face."

"Her eyes? Are they OK?"

"Yes. One bite was close to her eye, but it's fine."

"Where is she? Where do I go?"

"Just come to the emergency room. She's being taken there by an ambulance."

"Do you know where my boys are?"

"I think they're at your neighbor's house."

I hung up the phone and grabbed my car keys.

"I have to go—Lydia's in the hospital." I didn't even wait for Paul, my manager, to respond, I ran out. The parking lot, the drive—it's all a blur.

In the emergency room, Lydia was a tiny fairy surrounded by a throng of doctors yelling all the things you hear them yell on TV. Lydie was silent. A deer in headlights. And completely unaware of the horror that was at that moment what I knew to be the most beautiful face in the world. Her forehead was just gone. Her smooth skin ripped apart. If it had been almost anyone else, I would have had to turn away, but the blood and bone didn't bother me in the slightest. Her arms were bitten, her shoulder torn up—a big bite taken out of her gorgeous, olive-colored shoulder.

I moved right through the group of nurses and doctors hovered over her and sat down on the bed. Intravenous lines ran in and out of her every limb. You'd think she'd be screaming— I might be. But not a peep. She was happy to see me. Put her two little arms, covered in bandages, around my neck.

"How ya doin'?" I said in my most cheerful voice.

"I got bit." Her voice was sleepy and a little confused.

"Yes, you did, didn't you? But don't worry—you'll be as good as new before you know it. We're just going to stay here at the hospital for a while, OK?"

"Yeah. I got to ride in a amulass," she said.

"Very cool. Was it fun?"

"It was OK. I think it would be better if I din'nt have to lie down the whole time."

We had this conversation as doctors and nurses moved around her, poking her with needles and inserting tubes. She was amazingly calm. The ambulance driver, who had been watching quietly from the side brought over a teddy bear and gave it to Lydia.

"I promise that as soon as you get better, you can ride in the ambulance—and this time you'll get to look out the windows," he said.

"I have to pee," Lydia said hugging the bear. I couldn't believe this little girl, not quite yet four, hadn't just let go and peed in her pants.

"She can go to the bathroom if she wants," a nurse said. And just like that, all activity stopped as Tom picked her up and took her to the bathroom, IV and all. The trauma team, the doctors, nurses, EMTs had nothing to do while we waited for her.

"We have to take her into surgery now, Mrs. Shepherd," a nurse said. "Please sign here."

"Wait. What are they doing in the surgery?" I asked. My baby was going under anesthesia. An older gentleman walked over and calmly took the clipboard from the nurse.

"Mrs. Shepherd, I'm Dr. Oliver. I'll be the surgeon in charge of your daughter's procedure." He had gray eyes and thick, very white hair. He was the poster doctor for the AMA— the exact combination of reassurance and competence that you would want to have working on your child.

"We are going to have to try and reconstruct your daughter's face. We have to see what is still there and what we will need to reconstruct. Hopefully, if the skin is still there, her face will get back to normal very soon."

My mind was a blank. I hadn't really thought about her face being normal again.

"But she's going to be fine?" I wasn't even sure she was going to be able to live through the whole thing.

"Oh, she'll pull out of this just fine. Nothing critical was attacked." I hated that word—attacked. "Her eye wasn't injured. Her neck or anything else. I don't think the dog meant to kill her—I think he was playing, but no matter. We have been pushing a lot of antibiotics, and she is already responding to them well. No resistance at all."

"Well, she's never been on any kind of medication before . . ." I said, trying to participate in the conversation.

"Never? Not even an ear infection?" He sounded amazed. I still couldn't get past *attacked*. Who attacked her? How did she get in the dog yard by herself? Why was she in the dog yard by herself?

"No, I've tried to keep them away from systemic medicines," I said, still trying to sound coherent.

"Well, good. OK, then. I'm going to go in. You sign these; and you'll see, she'll be as good as new."

And there I was. Left standing there in the middle of a vacant hallway, while my daughter's savior went off to complete his saving. I was in shock. I had no idea where Tom went. I found him in the lounge. My hands were shaking. My heart racing. There was no excuse that would be good enough. No reason for this to have happened. I walked up to where he was sitting on a couch, watching TV.

"I am going to try and remain calm, but be warned it is not going to be easy," I said through my teeth. Every car he had ever wrecked; every oven he had ever left on; all of the small irresponsible incidents were racing through my mind.

"First, who was it?"

"Moose."

"Moose? How could it have been Moose? Moose is the sweetest dog in the world."

"Well, I moved him to keep him away from Pinocchio." Pinocchio was in heat and making Moose crazy of late.

"Where is Moose now?"

"He's with animal control."

"I don't want him back. How did Lydia get in the dog yard?"

"Matt and Lydia were outside playing."

"Alone?"

"Yes, in the front, but I guess they went in the dog yard."

I could feel my fingernails cutting into my palms. It was a strangely satisfying feeling. I pictured my hands around this man's neck.

"And?" I said.

"And, I heard Matt screaming, but I thought they were just playing so I ignored it. I was feeding Alex."

"You ignored it, I see." I will not scream in the hospital. I will not scream in the hospital.

"And then he wouldn't stop—so I finally went out to tell him to be quiet and that's when I saw it all—it was so awful, you can't imagine."

"No, I imagine I can't. How is Matthew?"

"They're at the Carters' from across the road." Matthew played with their son on a fairly regular basis, and I had talked with them a few times. We weren't exactly friends, but it was kind of them to watch the boys. I knew the boys would be safe there for the evening—if not anywhere else.

"OK. I'm going back to the surgery lounge. I am staying here tonight. You can leave." I had no desire to comfort this man. I had no sympathy. I was tired and mad and I wanted to see my baby. I walked away. Maybe I shouldn't have. Maybe I shouldn't have walked away from the man who once brought me an island for my birthday. But those days were long past. I sat up waiting in the deep, springless sofa of the lounge. Tom left. It wasn't hard to convince him to go.

I watched the clock. I watched the doors. I watched nurses come and go. It was late now, nearly midnight. I hadn't realized until just then that we had spent nearly four hours in the emergency room.

The doors finally opened. The clock said 3:00 A.M. When did it get to be 3:00 A.M.?

"She's fine," Dr. Oliver said. "She's up in her room. There's a large bandage over her forehead, and we had to cut away some of her hair because of the bites on the back of her head." I didn't know about those bites yet. It turned out that Moose had taken the back of her head into his jaws and probably tried to shake her head—maybe even snap her neck—so much for the sweetest dog in the world. I wanted him dead.

"All in all, she has well over three hundred stitches, and she will need to come back and get those taken out in a couple of weeks."

"OK—can I go see her now?"

"By all means. Marissa here will show you the way. And I'll see you in the morning."

The room was small, but private. Lydia slept with an IV and other monitoring equipment stuck to her. She had a net and bandages around her head. When we would take them off a few days later, some of her hair would come out in my hands in big, thick fistfuls.

I slipped into bed next to her, careful not to disturb the gear. This was not the first time I had shared a hospital bed with Lydia. She had been hospitalized once before. When she was three days old, I was visiting my parents and had Lydia cradled in my lap while I read the Sunday paper on the couch with my dad. I kept looking at her and rubbing her wee, little soft head. On one of the looks down to my sleeping newborn, I noticed she looked blue.

"Dad?" More than a little panic was evident in my voice. "Dad? Does she look blue to you?" This was the stuff SIDS was made of in my mind. My father immediately took Lydia and gave a couple of little puffs in her mouth. She cried hard and loud within a few seconds. We took her to the emergency room anyway. It was not our pediatrician's regular hospital, and the residents put her on every machine and poked her with every possible needle. She looked fine. She sounded fine. And I was beginning to regret my decision to bring her there. A quick call to our regular pediatrician, and he told the residents there to let us go—with the provision that he would look at Lydia the next day.

We went home. I kept Lydia near me all night. Everything

seemed fine and then, while I was home alone, of course, she turned blue again. I rocked her, walked her around, but nothing—no cry, no sound. Completely freaked, I gave her a small wallop on the butt—just enough to move her a bit, and she immediately cried. Relieved, I sat down on the couch and called Laura to ask her advice. Tom had the car, so I didn't want to rush and call an ambulance. I waited. I talked to Laura a few times. I watched Lydia. Watched her heart beat. Felt her pulse. Felt her breath with my hand. And then she did it again.

I called Laura, and she took all of us—Lydia, Matthew, her two kids, and me—to the hospital. I was so grateful to her. She called my parents who came to look after Matthew. They put Lydia and me in a room next to the nurse's station. It wasn't until weeks later that I realized that they were probably trying to keep an eye on me just as much as on Lydia. But I didn't care. I wanted them to fix her. They gave her tests. Put monitors all over her body and for three days we lived in a hospital crib. If I moved her the wrong way, even a little, her monitor would go off, and the nurse would rush in.

A few times, her heartbeat would go very low and set the alarm off, but while I thought she had stopped breathing, it turned out she was breathing shallow, whatever that means. The doctors told me she would eventually grow out of it. I got to take her home.

Now, I lay there next to her perfect little body and watched her breathe, just as I had almost four years before.

The nurse did pull out the cot for me, but I couldn't sleep so far away—even though it was just the other side of the room. I couldn't leave. She was so small, but so brave. Lydia is so different from me—from anyone that I have ever known— that she almost seems like she's from another place. She has an effect on people. She makes them kind, and they want to be good when they are around her. Well, she has this effect on everyone except for Matt, who just likes to get her angry—but that's good too, I think.

Her casual attitude toward the accident was almost frightening. She asked for a mirror, and I was so afraid she'd freak out that I didn't want to do it. But the nurse made the obvious point that if we didn't do it now then she'd either think it was really bad or she'd see her reflection somewhere else first and be unprepared. She already told everyone who walked in her room that she used to have long hair, but it was short now because she had surgery. She didn't sound proud when she said it but she also didn't sound sad—just matter-of-fact. She had long hair, now it's short. No big deal.

So with much trepidation, I presented Lydia with a handheld mirror.

"Now, before you look, there's something you should know," I said, placing the mirror facedown on her lap. She was in her hospital bed, her legs covered with the thin, off-white, hospital-issue blankets.

"I know Mom," she said. "Mooser bit me. I have stitches, right?"

"Yes, but you have kind of a lot of stitches—they're blue and they're in the shape of a big bite—kind of like an apple."

I picked up the mirror.

"Ready?" I said.

"Yes," and then she closed her eyes and held her breath.

She opened one eye. Then both eyes, very wide. She winced.

"Why did Mooser do it?"

"I have no idea. Do you want to tell me what happened?"

She shook her head.

"Can I watch *Sesame Street*?" And that was it. She was good. I kept waiting for questions, crying, anything. But they didn't come.

We walked down the hall to the playroom, accompanied by her robot friend ViVee, which was actually the IV attached to her arm, and she made no apologies for her bandages or her lack of hair. She walked proudly and talked eagerly. But if you walked into her room with a needle, you had better be ready for the tantrum of the century. She would have none of that needle business anymore, and who could blame her?

Two days later, the doctor released her. I was given instructions on keeping her stitches clean and was to report back in a month to have the outside stitches removed. She had several layers of stitches, nearly three hundred in all, and although some would dissolve, some had to be taken out. After a tearful thank-you to all the nurses on the floor, we had only one more stop before we could leave the hospital—the finance office. There, a kind woman explained that because I only worked part-time, I qualified for Maine Medicaid and could have all of Lydia's bills taken care of. In fact, I could have any medical bills for three months prior to her accident taken care of as well, but I didn't have any. This was one of the things that had been bugging me consistently since we had taken on this new lifestyle. Supposedly we were self-sufficient, but then when the shit hit the fan as it just had, we had to accept government help. Didn't sound very self-sufficient to me.

I dutifully filled out the forms, and we were on our way.

It was strange to read about her in the newspaper although they never mentioned her name, and I had refused to comment when the reporter called because I felt so completely guilty. I wanted nothing to do with the papers. I avoided phone calls and hoped that no one would recognize us.

On the way home from the hospital, Lydia and I stopped at the toy store to buy her a special toy. She wanted a Barbie. Being a thoroughly modern mother, I decided long ago that Barbie would never cross my threshold. But there is no saying no to a girl who just went through the worst possible horror—so, welcome Barbie. As a child, I actually had a Barbie township—complete with dream house, apartment building, pool, and convertible—but that was long before my feminist side developed.

We walked up to the counter to pay.

"What happened to your face?" a little boy asked Lydia. *Oh God*, I thought. *The stitches aren't even out and it's already starting.* I almost told the little boy to go find his mother and mind his own business, but Lydia piped right up.

"I got bit by a dog."

"That was you?"

"Yes." And then I swear she stuck her nose up in the air as she turned toward the counter. The boy had nothing else to say. To this day, Lydia handles inquirers with the same attitude.

Lydia's skin never burns in the sun; it gets the deepest natural tan I have ever seen. She gets it from my mother; my pale skin just gets blotchy in the sun. But her scars remain pink and then turn to an off-white—they'll never tan. Her hair will eventually cover the one side of her head that was bitten with Moose's lower jaw, near her temple. The back of her hair will look natural again. But her shoulder will always look ground up. It tans, but unevenly. And her arms will always bear the knot-like scars from the small bites that covered them. Her facial scar is less pronounced now (seven years later) than it was at three, but it is still obvious, and she has no desire to get it fixed.

With an injured child and the need to keep her and her

wounds absolutely clean, everything about the cabin now disgusted me. I boiled everything in water. I bought antibacterial soap, something I hadn't done since Matthew was born. The fact that there was no running water and wood dust and dirt constantly on the kitchen floor infuriated me now more than ever. Lydia wouldn't go to the outhouse because you had to walk past the dog yard. So we gave her a portable camping potty to use inside. Of course, I was terrified to let the boys outside now too, particularly Alex, so we all stayed inside all the time. I couldn't look at the dogs. I hated them. Moose was gone—killed by the police, a decision I had no part in. The other dogs, except for a couple of very special ones, represented only meanness to me. I wanted them all gone.

Each day for the month until her stitches came out, I had to wash Lydia's head in a Rubbermaid tub. It was sheer torture for me. It was all just wrong. People weren't meant to live this way anymore. She needed a nice bathtub and a safe place to play. Everything that I had liked about this life evaporated. And I was panicking. The walls of the cabin were closing in, the wood dust from the stove suddenly seemed more than dusty—it was disgusting. Each time I took myself or one of the kids to the outhouse, I cried. Each time I looked at a dog, I either cried from disappointment or gagged from revulsion at what I had let my life become.

"We are not leaving," Tom said. "You can't throw away our entire life here just because of an accident."

"Oh yes I can," I screamed. "And you can too. We can move away, give away the dogs, and have normal jobs like normal people."

"No. I won't," he said. "I don't want that kind of life, and I don't think you do either. You were fine before this happened."

"Well it did happen! And I won't subject our children to

it anymore. If you can't see that, then you're dumber than I thought you were."

"The accident was just that—an accident. It could have happened to anyone." When Tom got angry, he would go for a walk. He was heading out the door, but I wouldn't let him have the last word.

"No, Tom. It could not have happened to anyone. It would not have happened when I was here because I would have been watching them. I wouldn't have let them in the dog yard alone . . ."

"That's not . . ." He was going to say fair. I know he was.

"What's not fair—that poor you failed again? I'll tell you what's not fair, having a father who doesn't answer when you're screaming for your life. I am leaving. You can come or not, but I am leaving this hell hole."

And I did. Two days later, after Lydia got the majority of her stitches taken out, I picked up my last paycheck—about $150, plus tips the guys had saved for me after I left for the hospital, and a few donations—and I cashed it and packed up the kids. We were going to the beach. I knew things had to be better at the beach.

Part of me couldn't wait to go, the other part of me couldn't believe that this was how it was ending. After six years of marriage, eight years together, and three beautiful children, I was just allowed to walk out the door. Strangely, it didn't feel bad—just odd that it was that simple. I also wondered why it had taken me so long.

I knew, in my heart, that I was to blame for Lydia's accident. I knew it but I wouldn't admit to it. It pains me now to write it. And I will never forgive myself. Each time I see the scar on her forehead—what she now calls her Harry Potter scar—I know that it is my selfishness, my desire for something more that put her in such a precarious position. Moose was my dog. I raised him. The children's access to him was my fault. I should have insisted on a fence. I knew all of this, but it made it easier to go if I was blameless. It made it easier to leave that life—all of it—behind.

But Tom chose the cabin and his new life. He remained with the few dogs that were left. I couldn't believe it, but he let us go. He watched us drive away without a word to bring us back. Would I have stayed if he had spoken up? Begged my forgiveness? Vowed to go back to a more normal life? Probably. I probably would have, but I know in my heart that it wouldn't have taken long for something else to divide us. And I know the reason I left is because he was not capable of asking us to stay.

Five

I spent close to a hundred dollars on gas, food, and a motel room on our drive down Route 1. I spent the first hour driving silently, ignoring the children's play in the backseat while tears streamed down my face. As the flat roads of Aroostook County turned into the curves and hills of the coastline, I began to feel emboldened by my leaving. Just the sight of the ocean soothed my anxieties. Although the images of my married life raced through my head, the thought of this, my own independence day, became more and more enticing.

We landed in Stone Harbor, Maine, under cement skies, but as we drove into town, the sun came out. It felt like summertime here. Only a hundred and fifty miles separated the two towns, but it was like driving to a new planet. It was mid-May, and it was warm. I think it was snowing slightly when I left Belton.

I wound my car through town and parked at the bay. Something about Stone Harbor just felt right. Not too rich but not without thriving businesses. Some very nice houses and some that looked plain. Hippies, clad in the standard hippie uniform of Birks and tie-dye, were walking around downtown while tourists from New York and Massachusetts wandered with their overdressed children.

Matt, Lydia, and Alex, who was half walking, half crawling, played at the edge of the water while I sat on a log and watched. They looked happy. Lydia was remarkably well. Her stitches were gone, and her wounds healed quickly—a surprise to both me and the doctors. This was what I wanted to give them. If I couldn't give them cable TV and brand-new clothes, then I could give them this—days at the beach. And I would give them running water and electricity and a normal school in the fall.

We snuggled into bed for the night and I read the newspaper. I combed the classifieds for bartending and serving jobs and made a nice list. One thing Stone Harbor didn't lack in May was jobs in restaurants. Looking back through the rest of the paper, one particular article caught my eye. A man was opening a new restaurant called O'Hara's Pub and Grill and was restoring an old historic building in the process. They ought to be hiring, I thought.

The first thing the next morning, we went down to O'Hara's. The place was a disaster. There was dust everywhere, boards lying on the floor, leaning on the walls. And no one in sight. I sat the kids at a table covered in sawdust, ordered them to not touch anything, and went in search of someone. A man popped up from behind the bar. He was an older man and looked like he was in charge.

"Hi, can I help you?" he asked.

"Are you hiring?"

"Yeah, here . . ." He fumbled around under the bar and produced an application and a pen. "I'll go get Lyle for you.

He's the owner." I wiped off the kids' table and then my own and started filling out the application.

A different man appeared and sat down in front of me.

"Hi, I'm Lyle," he said. I shook his hand and smiled. He looked over my application and looked at me, and then he looked over the application again.

"Come with me," he said. I motioned to the kids to be quiet as I followed Lyle to the kitchen. It wasn't a large restaurant, so I could see them from where we were. The man from behind the bar brought them each a Shirley Temple, with enough cherries to start an orchard. Where, in all that mess, he found the makings for one, I had no idea.

"In here is the kitchen, and upstairs we have two dining rooms," he said. "We will be opening in two weeks—I know it doesn't look like it, but we will."

I nodded in agreement.

The nickel tour ended, and I was standing there looking stupid, watching the kids finish their drinks. Lyle walked over to the bartender, and then he walked back to me.

"Do you want to come to a wine tasting? We're having one right upstairs in about an hour."

"Um, sure," I said. "But—I have to bring these guys, I wasn't planning on staying long."

"Oh that's fine. They can play in the other dining room. It's right next to where we'll be. Don't worry, the upstairs is finished." I laughed along with him, trying to make a good impression.

"So, um . . . am I hired?"

"Oh, yes—you can start when we open on the twenty-seventh. We'll have a couple of training days before then." I didn't ask about pay—happy to have a job and knowing that most of my money would come from tips.

Wow, that was easy. I felt destined to be in this wonderful place.

The wine tasting was fun. The bartender from downstairs introduced himself as just Hogan. He was a large guy. Tall and big through the shoulders, but not body-builder big. His hair was cut in an incredibly short crew cut that made his blond hair look almost nonexistent, but the mustache and goatee on his face were dark red. I noticed that he had the strangest blue eyes I had ever seen. They were almost gray and stood out behind his wire-frame glasses. A few crinkles next to his eyes, coupled with his take-charge attitude, made me believe he was much older than I.

"First or last?" I asked, expecting him to offer the rest of his name.

"Last," he said. And that was it.

"You're not one of those people who refers to himself in the third person all the time, are you?"

He laughed, but a woman from the wine company, who was ready to begin the tasting, interrupted us. Another guy walked in with a mountain bike, which he parked under the stairs that went up to the dining room. He was wearing a bike helmet and glasses with flip-up shades. He had on a white shirt and a tie, but bicycle shorts on the bottom. He had beautiful legs. I don't normally notice legs on a guy, but I did then. I watched, stared really, as he put away his things and found his pants. I gazed with sheer delight—a delight I hadn't known in quite some time—as he walked back toward the bathroom to change. It had been quite some time since I had really noticed another man, and it came as kind of a shock.

"That's Jay," Hogan said, interrupting my daydream. "He's your boss when you're waiting tables."

"Oh," I said in my usual eloquent way. "Cool."

Lyle had brought a portable TV down from his apartment on what was the third floor of this massive building. The children settled into watching TV and eating sandwiches that I found for them at a nearby deli. They were being good—I wanted to go and tell them so, but far be it from me to wreck a good thing.

Hogan and Jay led the way to the upstairs dining room where we would learn about wine. It seemed so odd to be sitting there in a perfect dining room, with linen tablecloths and napkins, sipping varieties of expensive wine, sniffing the bouquet, swishing it around in my mouth the way I was being taught, less than two days after I had left a tar paper shack in the woods.

It was like emerging from a desert island to a real world full of people and experiences and as frightened as I was, I was eager to take part in all of it. After an hour or so of alternating wine with water so that I didn't get tipsy, I learned the difference between a merlot, a cabernet, a chardonnay, and all the rest. I could hear the kids getting restless, so I packed us up.

Not bad for my first try for a job, I thought as we descended the stairs out of the bar. I left that day, pleased to be employed, but terrified because I wouldn't have any money for another week. What would I do for a week?

We went back to the motel. While finding the job at O'Hara's was easy, what I soon realized was that staying in the tiny motel room was going to be impossible. Forty dollars a night seems cheap if you're only staying for one night. Once you start doing the math, though, $40 a night is $280 a week and thus $1,120 a month—hardly worthwhile for a bathroom, a dorm refrigerator, a hotplate, and two beds. With warm weather upon us, I figured that a summer of camping out couldn't be any worse than the cabin, and it would give us enough time to save up for an apartment of our own. But first, I thought, I should go visit my parents. They were only an hour away from Stone Harbor, outside Augusta. This I thought, would not only give me the opportunity to explain my new separation from Tom, but would stave off our impending poverty until my job started.

We checked out of our motel and drove the hour to my parents' house. Somehow I found the way although I had never come from the coast before. The first few hours in my parents' home are always the best. There is hugging and eating and drinking. The kids are fawned over, and I feel like I'm at home. It's a strange thing to be a visitor and still feel at home. I feel free to open the refrigerator and eat whatever I want, but I can't find the silverware or garbage bags.

We are set up downstairs on the floor in front of the TV, and I feel grateful for the place to stay. At the same time, as we sit around the dinner table, and I listen to my sisters relate their high school stories and ask my dad for money so they can go out, I feel the need to inflate my circumstances and sound successful in my new endeavor.

In retrospect, this was the time to ask for help, when I first left, with Lydia still newly scarred and my pain over leaving Tom still so fresh. I should have been crying and begging for help. But this is not me. I am terrible at asking for anything, and I can feel years of disappointment weighing me down.

"So, you moved to Stone Harbor," my father said.

"Yes, it's great. I remembered it a little from driving through, that time Mom took us to Bar Harbor, but I had no idea what a great little town it was," I said.

"We looked at houses around there when we first moved here," he said, "but I decided the commute was too far." He paused.

"Your mother said you have a job," he said.

"Yup . . . Matt stop kicking the table . . . it doesn't start until next week though, so I thought I'd come see you before I have to work all the time."

"Good, good, what are you doing?"

"Just waiting tables, but it's summer and there are plenty of tourists, so the money should be pretty good."

"Definitely. Will you keep looking for something else?" This was always the catch—would I find a real job? Something respectable that would give me good benefits.

"Um, yeah. I thought I might check out the newspaper and see if I could string for them and maybe that would put me in good for a full-time position." I'm lying. I've just come up with this just now, but it sounds really good, and that's the most important thing.

"That sounds great, Shell, I hope it works out. You could always go back to school."

"Yeah, I could," I said, thinking, like when exactly? With all that free time I have with the kids?

"Maybe night classes or by correspondence."

"That sounds perfect, I'll go to the library and see what I can find out."

"Where are you staying? Still in the motel?" This is it, I think, this is the time to ask for money for an apartment.

"Yeah, it's not too expensive, and I'll find an apartment soon."

"Tom's helping you out, I assume."

"Yeah," I said. *Chickenshit*, I thought.

"I never liked that boy," my father said.

"Dad!" Then under my breath, "You can't say that in front of the kids."

"Oh, right, sorry."

Why couldn't I do it? Why couldn't I just ask for the money? Because I had already blown two thousand dollars on winter stuff and dog gear. Because I had caused my parents enough pain through the years and admitting that Tom was off on his own and had not, in fact, supported us for quite some time was just too much. I wish I could say that there was some event, some trauma, in my childhood that would not allow me to ask my parents for money, but the truth is, there is nothing. They are not mean or selfish. If they had it, they probably would have lent it to me—OK, given it to me. The fact is that I was tired of having to ask for their help. I was tired of admitting that maybe my inspired decisions at the age of eighteen were the wrong ones. I just wanted to do it by myself. I wanted to prove to them, to the world, and to myself that I didn't need my parents, or a husband, to bail me out all of the time. I was also tired of feeling like a fuck-up.

I spent the week cleaning up after the kids, hanging out in the backyard, and waiting for my sisters to come home from school and my parents to come home from work. It's like a little vacation, but I can tell our presence is wearing thin. My dad has stepped on enough Legos to keep him from ever walking normally again, and my mother has about had it with the constant stream of Cheerios on the floor.

Still, they are outwardly good-natured. They never say anything, but they have begun to go to bed at 6:30, retreating, I am sure, to the silence of their own room. Meanwhile, my sisters, who are sixteen and eighteen, have taken to bringing friends home at all hours, climbing out of windows at night to get to weekday parties and begging me to buy them coffee brandy and Boones Hill Farm wine.

One week has begun to feel like a year and despite the logic that I should ask to stay here, it's not going to happen. I can't do this. I can't constantly walk on eggshells, worrying that the kids are making too much of a mess or are too loud. As much as I love my youngest sister, she is starting to drive me insane with her constant criticisms of how I discipline the kids. I don't even spank or anything, but if I so much as raise my voice and put them in a time-out, she goes over to my crying child and hugs them and tells them how mean their mother is. I hate that.

But I can't admit, out loud anyway, that Tom isn't going to help and that I have no money. Staying here would be admitting defeat and I am nothing but optimistic right now. Every night I talk vehemently about our future—trying to convince both them and myself that we are on the right path, that things are going to work out just fine. That I have finally gotten my life together.

Six

I drive back to Stone Harbor a few days before the restaurant opening and scope out the town for places to sleep at night. A couple of miles outside of town is a state park, which looks like it would be good, but it appears you need reservations to sleep there. I make a mental note to do that for later on in the week. There is also a private campground on Route 1, and then there's the little beach at the end of Main Street. I park at the little beach and let the kids run around while I contemplate sleeping there tonight. I decide that it is our best—and cheapest option—and so we will come down here when my training shifts are over. We also drive over to the truck stop I saw outside of town. We wander the aisles, looking for a decent breakfast for the next morning (granola bars) while I scope out the facilities.

There is a pay shower and a lounge for the drivers that I won't use. I also ask the guy at the counter if there is anywhere to fill up a couple of water jugs for tooth brushing, cooking, and the like. He points me to the back of the building and says there is a faucet out there I can use. It's easier than trying to get jugs under the faucets in the bathroom, and I don't want to fill them up at work. I buy three gallon jugs of spring water to get us started and will then refill them as needed.

Another problem is looming before me though. I've known about this problem for several days now but have been unable to cope with it. It's opening night tonight, and I don't know what to do with the kids while I'm working. My shift starts at 4:00 P.M., and I know it's going to be crazy. It seemed so easy during these last couple of days of training. We slept at the beach, cleaned up at the truck stop before going in, did our laundry at the Laundromat and headed back to the beach before nightfall. The kids played in the spare dining room, and everyone humored them. But opening night is a different story. They can't be there, and I have no idea what to do. I look at some of the ads for day care centers or moms who have day care businesses in their homes, but they are insanely priced. Matt and Lyd, who are potty trained, are $85 a week and at least $3 an hour if you don't go by the week. Meanwhile Alex is $100 a week because he's not potty trained and $4 an hour. That's almost $300 a week. Now, I hoped to make decent money at O'Hara's, but I'm not stupid. I know that even if I clear $100 in tips on Friday night, I might make only $10 in tips on Tuesday. And my $2.12 an hour is just a mere suggestion of a paycheck at the end of two weeks—and who can wait that long anyway? Formal day care is definitely out. I have pretty much planned on letting them sleep in the car while I am working; the nights are cool and the very small employee lot is right outside the kitchen door. But what about until then? Maybe I can convince Lyle to let them watch TV in the other dining room. I don't think he plans on using it tonight.

I am also facing another problem. I need a uniform. We

have to wear black pants, black shoes and socks, white long-sleeved, button-down shirts, and ties to work. I only have one pair of black jeans, and I'm not allowed to wear them.

I also have no money. I am expecting to make a pretty good haul this evening so I didn't worry about handing over my last few dollars to the truck stop this morning for our showers, water, and juice. I was also able to come away from my parents' house with enough food to last a week. They practically cleaned out their pantry for us. My parents are great at this. Whenever I moved into a new apartment, they always came calling with enough groceries to feed a small country.

I walk into the thrift store a few streets down from the pub and begin to look around. I find everything I need within a few minutes and watch as Alex starts to make friends with the proprietor from his stroller. I'm starting to think I might have a plan after all.

"Hi!" I say to the woman behind the counter.

"Hello," she says. "Did you find everything you need?"

"Oh yes," I say, "Thanks so much. But could I ask you a favor?"

"Hmmm?" She isn't sounding as receptive as I had hoped.

"OK, here's the thing. I'm a waitress at the new restaurant up the street, O'Hara's?"

"Yes . . ."

"Well, I need all this stuff for my uniform. . . ."

"I see . . ."

"OK, I don't have any money at all," I say, smiling, "and I was just wondering if I could take this with me for my first night, tonight, and pay you with whatever tips I make first thing in the morning?"

"Oh, honey, I don't know," she says. "I don't usually do that sort of thing. And how do I know you really work there?"

"Um, well, I guess you don't, really . . . but hey." Inspiration has struck again. "Why don't you come up tonight and see the new place, and dinner will be on the house?"

"Really?" she says. "I haven't been out in ages."

"Well, then it's about time," I say.

"All right," she says. "It's a deal. And tomorrow you'll pay me for the clothes?"

"Yes, absolutely—tell her, guys, we'll be back tomorrow."

"We'll be back tomorrow," Matt and Lyd chant, as instructed. Alex says something about "Ack oororow."

I haven't really gone too far over the line here. Lyle did say we could invite family or friends to the opening for a free dinner, but I didn't have anyone to invite. I'll tell him, and he'll be fine, I hope. Luckily, I have proven myself to be the best server and bartender (the cooks say even better than Hogan) in the restaurant so far, so I am sure if he knows my uniform was on the line, he'll consent.

Walking around town in the hot Memorial Day sun, I am still surging with anxiety over what to do with the kids.

We walk down to the bay, and I sit on some driftwood while the kids play in the surf. My mother gave us a full jar of peanut butter and honey. "Your sisters won't eat it anymore," she said, "they say it's too full of fat or calories or both—who knows anymore?" So we have lunch for the next week. We picnic here at the bay. Despite my pressing problem, I am really loving this. Camping isn't so bad, and living near the ocean is more than I could have asked for. I really love it. Something about the salt air and even the sand in my shoes just makes me feel good again.

I spot a girl who was hired at the pub just this week walking down by the water. Ally, I think her name is. She walks over to us; and Alex, who has suddenly needed to see who is coming to talk to his mother, runs to sit next to me. Ally is very tall, with long strawberry blonde hair and freckles all over her face. She wears a tie-dyed T-shirt and cut-offs.

"Hey," she says. "How are you guys?"

"Good," I say. "Are you excited about tonight?"

"I'm not working tonight," she says. "I guess they want you older staff members to make sure everything runs smoothly." I laugh, but her comment stings a little. Ally is only twenty or twenty-one, not much younger than my twenty-four, but she's right, I probably look years older. I certainly feel older.

"Oh, that seems strange," I say, "but hey, what are you doing tonight?"

"Nothing, really," she says.

"Would you want to hang out with these guys until about eight or nine? I'd split my tips with you." I offer this because, first I know the prospect of babysitting three kids without benefit of a television (or a house) might put her off, and second because I don't know how much I'll make, and I want it to be alluring for her.

"Yeah, OK, I like to babysit."

"Awesome. You can play with them here, and I have some stuff they can eat for dinner. I think the library is open until eight—they love it there, too."

"Yeah," she says, "but don't you want me to put them to bed and stuff?"

I decide just to lay it out for her. I don't feel shy about doing this with someone younger than me, someone I don't really know.

"Yeah, I'd love that, but we're camping right now until I can find an apartment, so they have to go to bed in the car."

"Oh, OK, that's cool," she says. That's cool? I think. Why

couldn't she be my mother? "So, like, I'll bring them back to the pub when they get tired?"

"Yeah, great. Here, let me show you all their stuff." I walk her to the car. I pull out Alex's diaper bag and show her the cooler full of food. The kids have already started to clamor around her and ask her to play with them, but we still have a couple of hours before I have to start work.

"Hey guys, I'm going to go and get some lunch," she says to the kids, "but I'll see you in a few hours, OK?"

"OK!" they yell.

"Thanks Ally, I appreciate it," I say. The great fortune and sheer luck of this encounter is not lost on me. Maybe, I think, someone is looking out for me. At least, I hope that's the case.

"No problem, see you later."

"OK, guys, let's get Alex set up for a nap!" I pull a blanket out of the car, along with a few picture books and a couple of juice boxes left over from the week at my parents' house. The beach is not very big and is bordered by a stand of trees, so if you park away from the water, you can get a nice bit of shade. I set the blanket up, change Alex's diaper, and lay him down. Lydia runs the diaper to a nearby trash can while I coax Alex into lying down. He does, fitfully, but by the time I am finished laying Matt and Lyd out on their own small blankets with their books, Alex is asleep.

Before too long, Matt and Lyd are asleep too. I could sleep, but naps have never suited me well. I always feel more tired after them than I did before. I stay awake, leaning on one hand and watching a few stray tourists walk by the bay. Stone Harbor's beach is not a busy one. It is more of a scenic overlook for the people who go to the more popular seafood restaurants. The more popular beaches are farther south. But I like it, and as I lie here, I realize that this isn't so bad. I can do this. Soon, we will have a place of our own, and we will make Stone Harbor our home.

Opening night is insane. All the dining rooms are filled, and there is a line out the door. I arrived at 3:30 P.M. to help set up and haven't stopped since. Everyone is trying to be happy and cheerful, but is obviously edgy and nervous so a normal question like, "How long for table twenty-three?" gets a response like: "Shut the fuck up, can't you see I'm slammed?"

I decide to wait for my food just outside the doorway to the kitchen so that I can hear the cooks and still be out of range for the wooden spoons that are bound to start flying. My legs are killing me from the full flight of stairs I have to lug each tray of food up, and subsequently bring the dirty dishes down, but I soothe the pain with the knowledge that by the end of the summer I should lose a bunch of weight. With everything that is going on—separation, homelessness, three kids—I still have time to look in the truck-stop mirror in the morning and shake my head at my stretch marks and still bulging belly.

By 8:00 P.M., Hogan asks me to cocktail waitress downstairs because the line to the bar is so deep no one can get through to order. Now, this is fun. I run around a small space, get people drinks, and they tip me each time. For every two-dollar beer, they give me three dollars. Suddenly my job doesn't seem so bad. I try to talk Hogan into letting me do this every night. He just shakes his very sweaty head.

I am constantly getting pulled in every direction from someone wanting a new drink, and so I have taken to standing at the service bar and yelling, "Hogan!" or "Jay!" when I need to put in an order.

"What are you doing?" Another waitress—Rose I think—asks.

"What do you mean?" I ask.

"I mean, how do you yell at him like that?"

"At who?"

"Hogan. How can you yell at him? He's so, I don't know . . . isn't he kind of gruff and mean?"

"Yeah, I guess, but I don't care. He never hears me if I say his name nicely." I demonstrate saying, "Oh Hogan," in a very sickly sweet voice. I get no response.

"See? But if I do this . . . Hogan! I need two Bud Lights!" Hogan appears almost immediately with two Bud Lights. "Then he comes right away."

"Thanks!" I say to Hogan.

"Oh," I ask Rose, "did you need something?"

"Um . . . yeah, a frozen margarita and a Ketel One on the rocks," she says.

"Oh, man, that might be too much for him—give that one to Jay." Hogan is still standing near us, so I know he can hear me. He smirks and then leans in close to Rose.

"Don't listen to her," he says. "She doesn't know anything. I'll get those for you right away."

Rose looks stunned by the sudden attention.

"Oh sure," I say, "you're only nice to the cute girls . . ." And I leave before he can say anything.

Before long, it's 9:00 P.M., and Ally brings the children back. I've been saving my dinner break so that I could put them to bed. I thank Ally and split my tips with her—about twenty-five dollars.

"Thanks," she says. "They were great and I made more than I would have otherwise. I'd be happy to do it again."

"Wow, you guys must have been abnormally good," I say to

them. They smile and nod their heads up and down. "OK, let's go set you up for bed." I give Hogan my tray and my tickets, take them to the bathroom, and lead the guys through the kitchen and out the backdoor. I parked the car right next to the backdoor and have set the back up so that the seats lay down. I put a comforter down for them to lie on and set their pillows up right behind the front seats. Despite the three dining rooms, the restaurant wasn't really that big, and I could easily make frequent checks on them. Earlier in the evening I had pulled Barb, the head cook, aside and informed her of my plan. She said she would check on them often. I'm not really worried about anyone seeing them back there because the lot is very small, only enough for three or four cars, and it is blocked from the street by a fence and substantial hedges.

I open the hatchback door of the wagon and help the kids climb in. They lie down, and I take off their sandy shoes in turn, shaking them out in the parking lot before placing them back in the car. I also wash each of their faces and hands with baby wipes, but I forgot about their teeth. I'll make sure they brush well in the morning and make a mental note to keep their toothbrushes in my backpack so next time they can brush in the restaurant bathroom. We don't bother with pajamas. They just sleep in their clothes, which I will change tomorrow.

I change Alex's diaper, and we talk about all the fun things they did with Ally. I'm about to read them a story and notice that they're almost asleep. At least the fresh air is doing them some good. Alex is between Lydia and Matt and so I wedge myself in between Lydia and the wall of the car for a few minutes. I didn't realize until just this moment how tired I am. I could fall asleep right here, but I have to go back to work. I rub each of their backs for a bit and then, when I am certain they're asleep, I quietly climb out the back and lightly shut the door. I walk around the car and peek in the driver's side window, which I have left open. A cool breeze from the bay is taking over the heat of the day, so I know they won't die of heatstroke. Still, I made sure Matt knew where the water bottle was in case they woke up, and I told them they could come in if they needed anything.

As I open the screen door of the kitchen, I am suddenly crippled by panic. Maybe this isn't a good idea. I shouldn't do this.

"Hey!" Barb says. "Are your kids all tucked in?"

"Yeah, sound asleep," I say. "They'll be OK, right?"

"Oh, yeah, they're fine. Don't worry. Me and Lex are right here."

While they're out there in the car, I'm a nervous wreck. I run between the bar—where I have since replaced Jay and am now working alongside Hogan—the kitchen, and the car. Every possible horrible thing that could happen to them is constantly running through my mind.

Even with the knowledge that what I am doing is for the best and knowing that the children are, indeed, safe, my anxiety still works on me like a jackhammer. Between every drink I make and every wipe of the bar, I am thinking: "What kind of mother would let her kids sleep in the car?" "What kind of mother would tend bar for a living?" "What kind of mother would take her kids from their father and think this is a better life?"

I imagine what I will tell social services when they come to investigate. I hope that I would rant about some political issue of expensive child care and low wages. "Do you know how much day care for three children costs?" I would yell. But what I really want to do is just get through this horribly long evening.

The churning in the pit of my stomach is eased slightly by a customer's request for an old-fashioned. I hate making old-fashioneds. Mashing up all the fruit on the bottom and mixing it with sugar—it's the slowest drink to make—and I hate trying to take other orders when I'm in the middle of mixing one. Unfortunately, I have noticed, they are also very popular with the crowd that this pub will apparently cater to: the over-forty crowd, visiting a quaint coastal Maine town. O'Hara's is unlike most of the other bars in town. The majority of them, if they serve food and try to appeal to tourists, have dated décor and are small and cramped. The others are dives, with loud bands most nights and plenty of twenty-five-cent tippers, appealing mostly to the locals. O'Hara's has a mahogany bar with brass rails. It is spacious with linen tablecloths on the tables, and Lyle has made sure that when there is live music, it's a string quartet or an Irish folk band.

Barb sits down at the bar, requests a Jack and Coke and calls it RVs on Parade.

I pass by Lex on the way out of the kitchen and he informs me that the children are still blissfully asleep. I am grateful for Lex's silent vigilance and jealous of the children's peace. Lex is a mystery. He immediately intimidated me with his spiky dyed-black hair, multiple piercings, and tattoo-laden arms, but he watched over the children after Barb and the other servers left without giving it a second thought.

"No problem," he said. "I'm right here anyway, and it'll give me an excuse to go out and have a smoke."

Who are these people, I ask myself, who have so readily and willingly let me into their lives and given me a hand? Ally, Barb, Lex, Lyle; each one made room for us in their lives. I was so used to everything being a problem. Tom always whined before I left for work, asking me how long I was going to be. I always had to lay out everything—dinner, diapers, stories for bedtime—before I left, otherwise he'd call and ask me a million questions—like, "Where are Lydia's socks?" But these people just let us in. Ally found the diapers on her own. Lex, I have a feeling, would have kept an eye on the kids even if I hadn't asked. I was homeless, but was suddenly starting to feel more at home than I ever had before.

Seven

A week goes by, then a month, and what I thought was a one-time deal on opening night has suddenly become routine. One of the girls from the pub, usually Ally, watches the kids during the first part of my shift, and they sleep in the car during the rest. It's still a gut-wrenching proposition each time, but at the same time, it's becoming almost normal. We have a routine of sorts.

We spend the days walking around town, going to the library, to the beach, and to the Laundromat. At night they hang out with Ally at the playground or the beach if it's nice and in the second dining room if it's rainy. The second dining room is only open on really busy nights like Friday or Saturday.

Tonight I am bartending with Hogan again. My tables upstairs have left, and Jay wanted to cut out early. Between being desperate for cash and wanting to impress Jay, I quickly volunteered for the shift.

Barb plants herself at the bar. When I first met her, she

struck me as a cross between a rough biker chick and Georgia O'Keefe. She dyes her hair a new color every week and sits at the bar every evening after her shift, smoking her unfiltered Camels. She stays at the bar late every night, keeping me company, and running out to the kitchen door to check on the kids for me, but not without pausing to yell at poor Lex.

On one of her multiple trips to the kitchen this evening, she checks on the children and then whips a wooden spoon at Lex. She smiles broadly at her perfect aim and sits back down at the bar. Her cloud of smoke joins the already thick haze at the ceiling and, as the evening wears on, the haze moves lower and lower until I am standing with my head in a cloud, ducking underneath it to locate the beer taps.

I wipe down the bar again and proceed to mash up the fruit for another old-fashioned.

"Your little ones are just dandy," Barb says as she walks back from the kitchen. "How do you get them to sleep so well? When mine were that age they woulda been sitting here at the bar or jumping off the tables."

"Must have been that whiskey I slipped into their Shirley Temples after dinner."

"Ah you. When're you gonna take one of these fine specimens up on their offer to take you out? You should stop worrying so much and have a little fun. Make yourself up a bit."

"Oh, I don't know. I think I've had enough of men for one lifetime. Not anxious to get going again. Besides, don't you know that if some man looks at me just right I get pregnant?"

Of course, the possibility of my becoming pregnant had diminished drastically since Alex had been born. I still don't use any form of birth control, but considering I haven't had sex at all since his birth—and let's face it, there is no prospect of me having it anytime soon—I'm not concerned about it. I figure if anyone is ever that interested in me, I'll go back on the pill, but at the moment I have more pressing concerns than my sex life.

Before Barb could argue in favor of my love life any more, the old-biddy theatre crowd comes through the door. The business of the evening takes over my anxiety as I fill orders for Bloody Marys and frozen margaritas. Between orders I keep running out to the backdoor, and thankfully all is well.

I sink back into the all too familiar driver's seat of the car after my shift. It's been several weeks since I began this "plan" of mine, and it's beginning to take a toll on me, both mentally and physically. The constant scrounging for a place to sleep, the heat and the uncomfortable car seat where I sleep (and drive and get dressed sometimes) irritates me to no end. The car reeks of sand and beach and sweaty kids. It's not a bad smell, but it makes the car seem muggier. I wince as I start up the car—I don't want the kids to wake up at the sound of the motor, and I need a new muffler. My plan is to stay down at the beach. It's a short ride right down the hill—not even a mile, and there is no sense in wasting money on a campground at 2:00 A.M. On weekends, though, we have taken to staying in a nearby campground, where for twenty-five dollars a night, there is a playground, swimming pool, and a shower included in the deal. We also cook out and roast marshmallows, a truly cheap source of entertainment since they're only seventy-nine cents a bag! There are grills for the public and I can easily showcase my fire-building skills—feeling good that I learned something valuable in the tar paper shack—without needing charcoal or lighter fluid. Matthew and Lydia are expert kindling gatherers, and the race is always on to see who can provide Mom with the biggest pile first. Ramen noodles with a package of frozen vegetables thrown in are a staple dinner; so are omelets. I try to stay away from hot dogs, hamburgers, and traditional grilling foods, because it would be too easy to rely on them and to fill the kids up with junk food all the time. I try not to eat too much when I'm with them. I'd rather they eat everything we have, and then try to pick at something while I am at the restaurant. I can usually make up a salad or find a burnt piece of chicken that no one else wants. We also get one free regular meal for each shift, so I'll grab that too. Fortunately, I don't usually get hungry until after their lunch. Even on the days I do get a little hungry, I choose to wait. It just seems more fair.

I pull up alongside the beach, so I can look at the water out my driver's side window as it rushes onto shore. Well, I always wanted a house on the water, I joke to myself, and now I have one. Each day is beginning to get longer than the day before it. Some days are good, and I feel fine with what we are doing; other days are long and tedious, and I hate myself for what our lives have become. The car has become uncomfortable, even though I am grateful for it, and I am constantly searching classified ads for a place to live.

Cramped in the fetal position in the front seat of the car, while the kids are stretched out in the back, I yell at God in my head. But what's he going to do? There are far bigger problems in this world than us living in a car. We have lived in the car for a month now, but we are healthy, we are strong . . . so I yell at my ex-husband instead. But again, I'm not expecting a lot of help from there either. I called him once but the phone was disconnected. I yell because it's the only thing I can do, because I feel powerless. I want someone else to be responsible for this mess I am in. Why does it have to be so hard? I am beginning to feel like all of this isn't such a good idea after all. That I should have just stayed with my husband. Maybe I'm not as strong as I had thought.

It's interesting, when you are deciding to start a new life, what kinds of things you deem necessary to bring along. I don't really have anything of consequence. A few of the kids' favorite toys, some clothes, some pots and pans, and some photo albums. When I was packing, I just grabbed stuff I thought I couldn't live without. It's funny; even though some of it isn't at all necessary, I still feel like I need it. It just makes the car more cramped. If I were practical, I would ditch it. But I miss the comfort of being in familiar surroundings.

I have also become religious about saving money. It's not something I was ever good at before, but I have suddenly become incredibly responsible about this, even though everything else I am doing seems very irresponsible. I take half of everything I make during the week and put it in a videocassette box in my glove compartment. Some days that is only ten or fifteen dollars, but other days it's fifty dollars or more. On the days I make a hundred dollars in tips, I try and put seventy dollars in the box, but that doesn't always happen. On those days, I usually feel the need to eat a pizza for dinner or sleep at the campground instead of at the beach. I really wanted to be in an apartment by now, but the search is more difficult than I imagined. I am absolutely committed, however, to having an apartment by the time Matt starts school in two months. The pile of cash in the videocassette box in my glove compartment is growing and, with a little luck, it will be enough for the security deposit and first and last months' rent required to get an apartment.

The apartments are so expensive here, much more than I thought they would be in a small town like this. Five hundred and fifty dollars a month can get us a decent one-bedroom, but the competition is extreme between the new executives being flown in to work for the new credit card company in town and little old us. I know $550 doesn't compare to rents in big cities, but when you're only making $2.12 an hour plus tips, it's a fortune. Soon, I'm afraid, there won't be anywhere left to live. For a town that only supported the tourism trade, fish canners, and those working at McDonald's, there isn't a lot of housing left for the three thousand or so employees of one of the biggest banks in the country.

Each day I search the classifieds and scan the local bulletin boards, hoping for the break that's going to get us into a home. I have enough money now saved for the first month and security deposit on a studio or one-bedroom apartment, depending on the "view" of the ocean—meaning no view at all. I call on the more promising sounding listings and even schedule appointments, but once I drag all of us to the appointment, the landlord usually takes one look at us and says, "Um . . ."

The other day I thought I'd found our place for sure. It was a nice little apartment in an old house. It was downstairs, a walk-out basement, and had a little backyard I thought would be perfect for the kids. You walked into the living room, the kitchen was in the middle, and a large bedroom was in the back. And it was only $450 a month. Perfect. This is it, I told the kids. This will be the place. I walked into the apartment, confident and cheerful. The kids were reasonably well-behaved (meaning they didn't flip any buttons or switches) while we took the tour. There was a new refrigerator, a good stove, a dishwasher. Heaven on earth for a family living in their car.

"So," the gentlemen who owned the building pointed to the kids and said, "are they all yours?"

I always get this question. Tempted to say, "No, this one I

found on the side of the road and this one I kidnapped." I just smiled a very pleasant, fake smile and said, "Yes, they're all mine."

"Oh," he said, halfheartedly showing me the bathroom.

"I love it," I said. "I'd like to rent it."

"Well," he said, "I have a few more appointments this afternoon. I'll give you a call."

"Um, OK," I said, confused. "I could pay you right now or put down a deposit?" I phrased this like a question, hopeful that he'd take us on.

"Well, I really like to get the first and last month's rent in addition to the security deposit."

"Oh, but the ad said just first month and security," I said.

"Yes, but," he said, "I'll be honest, I just don't think this is big enough for the four of you."

"I know, but we need a place to live, and I love the backyard—it will be fine," I said, desperately trying to convince him.

"I'll think about it, but I'd hate to rent it to you and then have you decide you need something bigger."

"I'll sign a lease for however long you want," I said, knowing this last-ditch effort would be fruitless.

"Yeah, OK. Well, I'll call you and let you know how the other appointments go," he said showing us to the door. Crushed, I shook his hand and guided the kids back to the car.

All night at the pub, whenever the phone rang, I jumped, praying it was for me. Hogan started to get pissed at me for staring at him whenever he answered the phone. It never was.

I have similar encounters with potential landlords all summer long. They keep telling me that their apartment is just too small or that they won't "allow" me to set my sights so low.

It's a real catch-22. I can afford a small apartment, but no one will let us live in it. But my car, for some reason, is just fine, even though it's smaller! At least the car is paid for, although it's not insured. Let's just hope that if I ever get in an accident, it's not my fault. No one, except for Lyle and Ally, knows that the kids and I are living out of my car. I have told everyone else that I am simply having child care issues and need to keep the kids near me. Lyle only knows because I didn't have an address to put down for my W–2. He let me use his. I also gave it to my parents so they wouldn't worry. It's embarrassing, and I don't want to deal with the pity that comes with telling people. I have enough things to worry about without having to constantly reassure people that the children and I will be fine. Mostly, I am just not sure that we will be.

I am also trying to be good and refuse to spend any money out of the potential rent stash. Tips were light tonight, as I expected them to be, so I refilled my three large jugs of water at the truck stop for face washing and teeth brushing before my shift. Fortunately, the kids do not have an aversion to going to the bathroom in the woods, so that makes life a little easier.

I close my eyes and lay my head on the steering wheel. My thoughts are interrupted by a strong beam of light on my face. I turn to look out the window and squint into the light. A loud knocking on the door startles me. Because of the light, I didn't see it coming. The light is turned down and a sheriff's deputy with a flashlight is now peering in the car at me. Matt and

Lydia wake up and are on their knees behind me. Alex begins to cry.

"Ma'am?" the deputy says.

"Um . . . yes, sir?" My hands are shaking. My heart is pounding. Could he take the kids away? Will he? What do I say we are doing here?

"What are you doing here?"

"Um . . . sleeping?" I phrase my response like a question. I have only been pulled over by the police once before. That officer asked me if I knew why I had been pulled over. Why do they always ask questions like this? What do they think I am going to say? "Um, gee, officer, is it because of the shotgun under the passenger seat or the marijuana in my glove compartment?"

"You can't sleep here."

"Why not?" I'm not trying to be cheeky. I really want to know why. There's no sign posted. There are no hours at the beach as far as I know.

"Because you can't."

"But it's public property, isn't it?"

"Yes, but . . . hey. I know you from somewhere?"

"Yes. Did I wait on you the other day?" He actually asked me out, too, but I hesitate to mention that.

"What are you doing here?"

"Look," I say, in my most cheerful of voices, "we just need to camp out for a while until I save enough money for an apartment. I promise, I'm not going to do anything."

"I know, but . . . there are a lot of tourists here this time of year . . ."

"We'll leave early, I promise."

"If we catch you down here . . . sleeping, that is . . . after

7:00 A.M. I'll have to cite you." Cite me for what? Sleeping? Not wishing to press my luck, I reply, "OK. Thanks."

"All right. I guess I'll see you soon. Be careful, and please try to find a place to live."

"I'm trying, I swear."

"OK. Good night. Good night, kids." Matt and Lydia say "Good night," but Alex, who had quieted down to a soft whine, starts to cry even louder. Great. Now I'll never get them to sleep.

"All right, guys, lie back down," I say. They lie, but they're not happy. Alex is still upset, and Matt and Lyd are acting crazy. Giggling incessantly and poking each other.

"Guys, chill. We have to wake up early." Great. Now I am whining. I go to the Rubbermaid tub that has our books in it, and I find a copy of *Goodnight Moon* and a copy of *Green Eggs and Ham*. Every night for the last three weeks, my shift at the bar has begun at 3:00 P.M. So for a few hours, the kids have a great time hanging out with Ally or playing in the other dining room, but once 8:00 P.M. rolls around, it gets to be time for them to sleep. Unfortunately, I still have four or five more hours worth of work to do. So, I take my dinner break and sometimes I drive around until Alex falls asleep. It doesn't take very long. And then I park in the lot behind the kitchen and read to Matt and Lyd for about twenty minutes. It doesn't take long for Lydia to fall asleep, but Matt is another story. He's my watchdog and worrywart. He will sit and talk for hours if you let him. So on the nights when he has a particularly tough time, I rub his back and sing "Take me out to the ballgame," his favorite lullaby. Nine out of ten nights he'll fall right asleep, and I can slip out and go back to work. But not always.

One night he shocked the hell out of me by showing up at a

table and asking for a drink of water. Another time, all three of them came in to inform of me of Alex's poopy diaper. Got a big tip off that table. But they don't do it every night, and so far I have been fortunate in the fact that no one has complained. It's a tenuous position to be in, I know, but available babysitters are few and far between in this town. I keep looking, but the cheapest rate I've found is $3 per hour per kid. That's $9 an hour. Some nights I don't even make that much.

So back to the car they go. And I'll get Jesse, a young waiter, to keep an eye on my tables, and I'll sit with them for a few minutes, or change a diaper while they go back to bed. And they do. Maybe they understand that I need them to be-cause they very rarely give me any problem about it. When they do show up in their sweatpants in the middle of the night at one of my tables, teddy bear in hand, it usually lends quite a bit to my conversation with my customers. Mostly, they look at me and say: "How old are you? You can't be old enough to have three kids."

"I am Sam . . ." I begin, and before both books are done, both Alex and Lydia are back to sleep. Matt's still awake and wants to talk. We talk about kindergarten, which he'll be starting soon.

"Will Daddy come to school?" he asks.

"Probably not," is my tired reply.

"Why not?"

"I don't know, Sweetie. He's just busy and he still lives pretty far away."

"Oh."

"But I'm sure he'll try."

"Could we ask him?"

"Sure. But how about tomorrow? I'm sleepy now."

"Yeah."

I fall asleep with my head on the steering wheel.

"Mom?" My eyes are heavy and even with the gearshift in my back; I don't want to open them.

"Mom? The alarm is going off," Matthew said.

"Ugh . . . Oh, yeah, OK," I reply and then I slam my hand against the Mickey Mouse wind-up clock on the dashboard. "Let's get going."

Matthew woke up Lydia and Alex, and the three of them struggled to get dressed within the confines of the backseat. Although the days are hot, the mornings are quite cool by the ocean. The children are experienced now at getting dressed inside the car. They try and stay underneath the covers because to turn on the heat would mean to turn on the loud car and no one wants that. Legs are flying up in the air. Socks are tossed about. It's the morning jumble, and I am beginning to hate it, but it is kind of funny to watch. While they get dressed, I sort the bedding into the containers. I saw an infomercial once at the bar about a bag that you could place bulky items like sweaters and comforters in and then you attach the contraption to your vacuum and you suck the air out of it so that the stuff will store flat. My current storage plan is to stand on a pile of comforters in the Rubbermaid container and then try to slip out easily while simultaneously putting the cover back on.

"Hurry up and get dressed, you guys," I say. "Mama needs a shower."

I absolutely refuse to go without a shower. The only time I might consider it is on a Sunday when I don't need to be anywhere, but every other morning, without fail, we head to the pay showers at the truck stop, and I start the day looking like a normal person. Everyday, I make one of the kids hop in with me. The other two brush their teeth in the sink and play with wall-mounted hair dryers while we shower. This day is Alex's day. He hates showers. I try to hold him on my wet hip and wash his hair at the same time, but I get a fistful of soap in his eyes, which will only serve his memory and make him scream even louder the next time he is due to be cleaned. I decide to invent some sort of waterproof sling that will enable a mother to bathe her child in the shower and then I think, *who on earth would need such a thing besides me*? I laugh to myself, thinking of all the homeless-person convenience items I could dream up, which my target market could never afford to buy, not to mention that I could never afford to actually make them. *How about a house, Michelle? That would be the top seller*—sometimes my own brilliance slays me.

After Alex and I are sufficiently dried and dressed, we all head out to the convenience store. It's time for breakfast. Wandering through the store, I decide that it's more expensive to be poor than to be rich. Because we don't have basic things like a refrigerator, I can't buy concentrated juice for a dollar and make a pitcher to last for a couple of days. Instead I have to buy individual servings at a dollar apiece. The children have developed a taste for water.

Armed with our cereal bars and bottles of orange juice, we load up in the car. God, I'm starting to hate this car. We keep our things organized, if that is what you can call it, in a series of three Rubbermaid containers in the back of the station wagon. The containers are a remnant from the cabin. One of them is melted on one side because I left it too close to the woodstove while I was taking my shower. The rest I used to keep dog gear in and even though I have washed them out about ten times with the hose behind the truck stop, they still smell a little doggy. When we go to sleep, I place the containers outside the car and lay the seats down. In an effort to appear "normal" in town, I try to hide as much as possible in my giant Tupperware.

Eight

B y the end of June, I have had it. I keep spending more and more money on campgrounds and showers and juice and buying lunches out when it's too hot to cook or too hot for me to care that I'm spending the money. Some days I just drive us up to the McDonald's and for fifteen dollars we can all eat, and the kids can play at the playland for two hours. I can actually sit and read a book. I smile at the other mothers and pretend to be normal until it's time to leave again. These trips to McDonald's have become my guilt splurge. They are for all of the days we walk to the store and I have to say no thirty times to the kids before we leave.

I feel terrible saying no all of the time. Sometimes I feel like it's the only word I say. We'll be walking through the grocery store and I'll be figuring out in my head how much food I can get for the twenty-five dollars in my pocket, hopefully leaving at least five dollars for gas and maybe five or ten dollars to put in my savings account in the glove compartment.

I decide to apply for food stamps, thinking that the extra

help would allow me to save more for housing. It's difficult. Sometimes I go all week with consistently only five or ten dollars in my pocket, but I've become creative and it's doable most of the time. Usually, I'll make eighty or a hundred dollars on Friday and Saturday nights, so that hundred dollars will last us well into the following week, but by Tuesday or Wednesday, after a couple of loads of laundry, a few nights in the campground, gas, and food, it gets harder.

I'm still learning how to budget and sometimes get so fed up that I take us out to dinner. I usually regret it by Wednesday when I realize we'll be eating ramen noodles for two or three days. I've become an expert at making oatmeal at only ninety-nine cents for a few days' worth on a pan over the grill at the campground and sweeten it with sugar packets I steal from the convenience store. Yes, I confess, I do this—sugar and sometimes the little packages of salt and pepper—but that's it. If a store in Maine is charging for these now, it's partly my fault and I apologize.

Lunch is almost always peanut butter and jelly. Jelly stays cool in my little playmate cooler, even when the ice has melted and I don't feel confident keeping anything like mayo around. My fragile stomach has a great fear of salmonella. I'm actually quite impressed with my frugality skills. Years of poverty have made me the queen of shopping. I am never fooled by coupons that promise fifty cents off a name brand when I know the generic is larger and cheaper, and I am never tempted by individual servings and things that pretend to have fruit in them—like fruit snacks, which are really just a clever way to disguise what I always thought were gummy bears.

The kids have learned not to ask for these treats and know

they will go further with me at a grocery store if they ask for a quart of strawberries—real fruit—than anything with a cartoon character on the box. But I get tired of saying no. Even to things like strawberries, because they are just too expensive sometimes.

Each time, before we walk into the grocery store, I remind the children that we are only buying certain things. I show them my list, which has things like bread, milk, bananas, apples, cereal bars, ramen noodles, juice boxes, and maybe spaghetti and a jar of sauce on it. Desserts are rare, but I can usually afford a box of graham crackers, which can be both a snack and a dessert. Even though I have told them a thousand times that we are only getting certain things, walking through the store goes something like:

Matt: "Cool, Fruit Loops is giving computer games free in the box." Even though we don't have a computer, there is one he can use at the library.

Me: "No."

Lydia: "Can we have Oreos, just this once, please?"

Me: "No."

And then Alex, who isn't really talking yet, will grab a bag of something like gummy worms off the shelf and put them in my cart. He also grabs pudding and pistachios. Since he's never had pistachios, I think he just likes grabbing for things he can reach. Then, when I put them back, he howls like I'm the most abusive mother in the world and just when I think that someone is going to call the police on me for Alex's howling, Lydia decides that she's mad at me for not buying the Oreos and sits down in front of them, refusing to get up. Matt, in the meantime, is swinging the jug of milk around so that it just misses an older lady and she turns around and glares at me.

"If you don't slap that child, I will," she says.

92

I grab the milk from Matt and deliberately place his hand on the cart.

"Don't move until I say so," I say. Then I have to focus on Lydia, but Alex has just figured out how to unbuckle the seat-belt in the cart and is now leaning for another box of God knows what, so while I am catching Alex and placing him on my hip to be held there until I can check out, I have to have Matt help me push the cart so that I can half drag Lydia on her bottom across the floor. She helps out occasionally with a push of the foot, but she is basically just sliding on her butt, determined to get those Oreos. I would have caved, but first it would have cut into the rent stash and second, I'm on a mission now for her not to have Oreos after all of this.

I finally make it to the check-out line and after two minutes of playing put-the-food-on-the-conveyor-belt-and-put-the-candy-back-on-the-shelf, I shell out my meager twenty dollars and finally get the children into the open air.

I can't wait for the day when I only have to play this game once a week, being able to stock up, rather than every other day so that nothing goes bad in the car.

I cheerfully walk into the Job Center—doing my best to put on an air of the kind of person who is "just down on my luck—not a perpetual welfare case." I do not want to be associated with the really poor people. I am not really poor. I just don't have a house. I take the clipboard full of forms, while Matt and Lydia take Alex to play with the three broken toys into the corner of the waiting room. I take out my date book and fill in the numbers from my driver's license, the kids' social security cards, and my previous address: Hell, East Dumbfuck, Maine.

It's a drab room with dirty beige carpeting. I give up on

trying to get Alex to sit in a chair instead of on the floor. I hate dirty knees on kids, unless they have been outside playing. I hate that poor-child look and am determined that no matter how poor we are, we will never succumb to the idea of being poor. If we give into that, then there is no turning it around from there. I am unsure of a lot of things right now, but that is not one of them.

The hours wear on in the dingy room, and the heat is becoming unbearable. So is the smell. It isn't a bad smell, but a worn-out one. The smell of people who are tired. The smell of medication and diapers. All these smells, combined with the cheap coffee I had for breakfast, is beginning to make me nauseous. I start scanning the room to get an idea of where the nearest bathroom might be when finally a bird-like old lady primly calls my name. I wipe away the sweat that has been forming on my cheeks and pick up Alex. We follow the lady into the mysterious back office.

The office is like a maze.

"I hope there's a piece of cheese at the end of all this," I say. Matt laughs. Ms. Vande Hei gives me a wan little smile as she escorts us into her tiny office. The office looks absolutely unlived in. There are no pictures on the walls or on her desk. The walls are beige, the carpeting is beige, and if there hadn't been molding on the floor, there would have been no way to tell between the two.

After typing the information from the forms into her computer for what seems like an hour, Ms. Vande Hei smoothes her pleated skirt, looks at me, and says, "I'm sorry, but you don't qualify for assistance."

"You're kidding me," I say.

"No. I don't kid. According to the computer, you and your children should be fine on the income you currently provide," she says. "If you like, I can set you up with a financial counselor, and she can help you budget your money better."

Fighting back tears, I meekly reply, "Unless she has a lead on a house, she can't help me."

I am seething with anger as I pick up Alex, hitch him up on my hip, motion to Matt and Lyd and practically run out of her office. It would be a great exit but I make wrong turns and can't find my way out of the damn building.

"Of all the fucking," I mutter under my breath. "Sorry, Alex."

"Eat lunch pwease," he says.

All I can think is *Why not ask old bird face back there, she can probably buy you lunch?* Finally I find the door that leads outside and I stop and take a deep breath. I want to rant. I want to rave. But I don't. I don't want the kids to think that anything is really wrong. And I guess it's not. We're not too desperate—it's still summer, there's still time.

I want to tell Ms. Vande Hei to piss off. I want to ask her if she has any idea what it's like to wake up every hour on the hour not only to check on the sleeping children in the back of the car, but also to adjust the gearshift that is jammed in your stomach for the fifth time. I want to know why it's better—in terms of qualifying for assistance—for me to have a house and all the bills that go along with it and no food—rather than no house, no bills, and no food. I am convinced that the problem was that I was honest about how much money I had saved. If I had only lied—well, I'd be committing welfare fraud—but more than that, I'd be able to afford food and save up more money for a place to live. That seems to be more important right now than telling the truth about the stash of ten-dollar bills in the glove compartment.

We walk back to the car. I'm sick of that car. It is alternately both my savior and my menace. I don't have to work today, so we walk around town. I love to walk through this town. We go to the library, the ocean, the Laundromat. People smile at us. They don't know how poor we are. They don't know we live in our car. We look normal walking around town. We feel normal.

Inside, I feel like the biggest loser ever. How is it possible that this is what my life is supposed to be like? I went to American University! I worked in the U.S. Senate! I am smarter than this—I have to be.

But maybe I'm not. What kind of mother would put her children through a life like this? What kind of parent would make her children endure a life without . . . without what? Without television? Without electricity? Without space? Just without. I am sickened by my selfishness. How dare I think I could provide a better life? I'm a loser. There are people who didn't finish elementary school who provide better lives for their children.

"I'm thirsty," Matt says, and of course, Alex and Lydia chime in with "Me too!"

"We have some water in the car," I say.

"I don't want water anymore," Matt says. Alex and Lydia don't say anything, I think they suspect a battle they should stay out of.

"That's all we have right now," I say in my most Mary Poppins-esque tone. "If you're really thirsty, you'll drink it." I hand Matt the bottle. He drinks a small, test sip.

"It's warm," he says and then he gulps down more.

"But are you still thirsty?" I ask.

"No," he says, passing the bottle to Alex and then Lydia. I put the bottle back in my knapsack, which doubles as my purse and all-purpose beach bag, and continue to walk.

We head to the library. The library has a great, and free, story time, where the children can be entertained and I can walk the stacks in peace. I get a little tired of being a walking Vaudeville show sometimes.

After the morning with Ms. Vande Hei, I am actually too tired to do any reading and so I sit, with Alex in my lap, on the floor and listen to a Mary Poppins wannabe read to us. I am falling asleep. I could so just fall asleep.

"Hi," a cheerful voice next to me says.

"Hi," I reply, trying to look awake. A cute young woman is next to me. She is holding a two-year-old in her lap.

"What's the story?" she asks.

"*Madeline Takes Manhattan*, I think," I say. She laughs. At least she knew I was kidding. "No, it's *Good Night Moon*, and it's putting me to sleep."

We continue with the normal mom conversation: "How many do you have?" "What do you do?" It turns out that Diane is considering taking on some babysitting work.

"I don't really need the money, my husband is an OB," she says. She's not bragging, just providing information. "But Dylan here could use some friends to play with."

"Would three kids be too many to take on?"

"Oh, do you need a babysitter?"

"Well, yeah, actually. You see we're new in town, and I'm all alone with the kids. I've been working nights and . . ."

"Where's your husband? Oh, I'm sorry—are you married?"

"Well, I was . . ."

"Are you divorced? Oh, that's just . . ."

"No, I'm not divorced."

"Oh God, I'm sorry . . . oh, of course. I'd be happy to babysit. What's your phone number? Or tell you what, why don't you come over to my house tomorrow afternoon? We'll have lunch and the kids can see if they like my place." I'm thinking, you have a house, they're going to like it just fine. But I don't say that.

"OK. That sounds good. Do you want to give me directions?"

She gives me directions and we agree to meet.

"Great!" She was so happy. "I can't wait—this will be great." She was too happy. Or maybe I was just too tired. Was I ever that cheerful? If I was, I can't remember it.

When story time is over, I introduce the kids to her and tell them we're going to her house tomorrow.

It's not until I start strapping the kids into their car seats and I'm replaying our conversation in my head that I realize what Diane must think. She thinks I'm a widow. I might as well be.

The evening is long. I hate trying to keep the kids happy and occupied while simultaneously trying not to drive myself insane with boredom. We go to the playground. Matt and Lyd play while Alex takes a nap in the backseat. I sit on the hood of the car, ready to pounce if one of the kids needs me, but able to see Alex from my perch. Lydia brings me leaves and flowers. Matthew brings me pinecones. I check my watch. The minutes crawl by. God, what I wouldn't give for a television. Just something to keep me from thinking. I think too much. If I could just stop thinking, maybe I could enjoy my life. Or at least get some rest. The only time I'm not thinking is when I'm working. I like not having time to think. It's restful.

I wave and clap as Lydia comes down yet another slide. Matt is swinging on his own and trying to scare me with his "Look, Ma, no hands" routine, but I just smile and wave.

The kids are done playing—or rather, I'm done watching them play. An hour and a half at the playground is about my limit. You can only smile and clap as a child goes down a slide so many times before it starts getting really old.

We go to the campground. I hand my twenty-five dollars over to the nice man in the booth and we wind our way through the happy, vacationing families to our home for the evening. Spot number 45.

Then Alex is awake and waddles through the woods with Matt and Lydia gathering sticks, pinecones, and dry leaves for our fire. I pick up some larger logs from the pile near the bath-house, for use by the customers.

I build a nice fire, and we all sit and watch it grow. I get some water from the pump and fill our pot for ramen noodles. I forgot to stop for frozen veggies, which I usually put in with the noodles. Actually, I didn't forget. I just didn't feel like stopping again. So I dig out a bag of apples and bananas and make an impromptu, if very uninteresting, fruit salad for us to pick at while the noodles cook. I should get one of those solar cooker things. Maybe I could bake something, like biscuits or rolls. No, never mind. I want an apartment with an oven. I've got to stop trying to make the camping life better. I want a real life.

We eat. And then I put a larger log on the fire, and we go to the bathhouse to wash up. We wash our dishes with a bar of Ivory soap and a washcloth. We stack them wet and then carry them back to the car. I dry them with the beach towel I use for showering and then put them back in their Rubbermaid container.

It's six o'clock. Great. Three more hours to kill. All right, I have some marshmallows left. We can do that. Another half hour gone.

We take a walk and say hello to some of the nice people who are on vacation. We tell them that we're on vacation too.

What a liar I've become. In two days I've gone from homeless single mother to vacationing widow.

It's a hot night. I douse the fire with water, and the kids squeal with delight at the steam. I open the back of the car and lay the backseat down. I sit with my feet dangling out of the back while they squirm into place. There is no changing into pajamas. There's no point, really. We just sleep in our clothes. I put a light blanket over them, but they tell me it's too hot.

I read to them, but it's not working. We are all distracted by our sweating. There is no breeze tonight and the sun is still peering slightly through the pine trees. We could lie on the ground, but I don't really have anything to pad it—besides, I don't think it would cool us down any. I rub their legs, and we look at the stars. It's surprisingly quiet, considering all the people who are staying here. The smell of campfire permeates the air and makes us feel hotter even though we are not close to them. We hear people whispering as they walk to the bathhouse, their feet crunching the gravel and pinecone paths.

One by one, the kids fall asleep. Alex first. The heat always makes him tired. Lydia next, although she is the most resistant, always claiming that she's not sleepy.

Matthew talks until he can talk no more and finally drifts off. I climb into the front seat and lie on my back across the two bucket seats. I rearrange the gearshift slightly so that it's only jammed into my side. My feet dangle out the driver's side window. I grab a pillow and put it behind my neck. It makes me feel hotter, but at the same time it absorbs the sweat from the back of my neck. I'm not sure which is better.

We wake up in the morning in a sweaty pile. Alex's leg is over my neck. One of Lydia's arms is over Matt's face and the other is over Alex. Somehow Matthew has turned completely around during the night and has a leg over Lydia's stomach and a leg out the window.

It appears to have cooled off during the night but I lack the desire to start another fire, so we walk—the four of us—toward the camp store to get some milk for a box of corn flakes I bought. I love cereal, but the expense of it makes me cringe. I can't believe that someone can justify charging four dollars for a box of puffed sugar. But corn flakes always make the cut. I can usually find a behemoth box for under a dollar, making it my breakfast of choice when I have a place to eat breakfast.

We sit at the picnic table and eat from the four bowls I found for a quarter at a yard sale. The spoons were in the free box. Then we do our camp chores. We sort through clothes, making three piles: very dirty, wearable dirty, and clean. I try and keep the very dirty distinctly separated from the clean by putting them in plastic garbage bags. Although I hate keeping our stuff in garbage bags because it makes me feel like the proverbial bag lady, I love garbage bags. You can get almost anything into one. We also all have a lovely aroma about us, a little something I call Eau de camp that is basically a mixture of wood smoke, Deep Woods Off, and sweat. I put all the clothes we wore last night into a "very dirty, definitely not wearable until they see a heavy-duty washing machine" garbage bag, and search for something more suitable. We take our showers. When we are at the campground, everyone gets one because we aren't paying per shower.

Though we can't afford a home, I notice that my children have an obscene amount of clothes from designer stores like The Gap. This is not from shopping in those stores, but from scouring yard sales, a routine I picked up from my father years ago. We spent many weekends together when I was a child going to yard sales and flea markets, and I am glad that some of his negotiating skills have rubbed off on me.

The yard sales I go to are the ones in nice, but not too nice, neighborhoods, where the folks are looking to empty the crap out of their houses. The best ones have kids two or three years older than my own, so the owners are sick of looking at all their kids' old stuff, and they have already given up trying to give it all away. These people don't care if you give them twenty-five cents for a shirt or ten cents; they just want you to take it away. But they also have the common decency not to try and sell crap that's broken or torn. These are true yard sales, and they are my savior.

Finally we are clean and ready to begin our day. We load up and pull out of the campground. It's 10:00 A.M. and we are to meet Diane at noon. We wave a good-bye to the man in the booth and then head for the Laundromat. We put the clothes in, walk up to the dry cleaners to pick up Jay's shirts, and then walk up to O'Hara's to see what my schedule looks like and to drop off the clothing. I offered, in a somewhat weak moment the other night, to pick up Jay's shirts because I knew I was going by there, and I hoped to make myself indispensable and thereby somehow attractive to the most gorgeous man I'd ever seen. Plus, I was weak and feeling needy.

Hogan is there, smoking a cigarette in front of the pub, as always.

"Whose shirts are those?" he asks.

"Jay's," is my shameful reply.

"You pick up Jay's shirts for him?"

"Sure, why not? He can't be here during the day when the cleaners are open, and I like him."

"Don't you mind being used?"

"I'm not being used. I offered."

"He's gay, you know."

"He is not."

"Swear to God."

"You're crazy. He is not. And even if he is, what does it matter if I get his shirts?"

"Doesn't matter to me a bit." Hogan is such a pain. I swear he lives to irritate me. He picks on me constantly at the bar. Not that I mind. I like the informality and the tossing of insults at the bar. But Hogan and I can really get into it. A battle of the minds, if you will. Or more, a battle of the cynical, always trying to one up each other and have the last word. Hogan irritates me to no end, but for some reason I really like him. He actually had the audacity one day to tell me he was the smartest man I'd ever meet. It really pissed me off because my father used to say the exact same thing.

We go into the pub and look at my schedule for the week. It appears I have to work tonight. This is something I wasn't planning on, but I'm not completely surprised. This often happens in restaurants. People erase names and change schedules without asking and if you don't think to check, you can be accused of not showing up for a scheduled shift. I just hope that Diane really will take the kids on. I don't know if I can do any more nights in the car. The anxiety and stress of it all is wearing on me. Besides, it will be too hot for them to sleep in the car, and I hate asking Lyle if they can sleep in the other dining room again. On several occasions when it has been too hot, Lyle has been nice enough to let the kids sleep in the banquet room while I am working. I pack them up in the car when my shift is over. But I hate asking. I can also tell that Lyle has a bit of a boss's crush on me and that he will do almost anything I ask. It is tempting to take advantage of this, but I don't want to ask more from him than I have to. Still, it is nice knowing that there is someone in the world who will go out on a limb for me occasionally—even if it is a wee one.

We leave the pub with a quick wave to Hogan.

"Hey!" he calls after me. "Wanna get my shirts for me tomorrow?"

"Nah. You're not cute enough." I smile and flip my hair as I grab Alex's hand. Did I really just flirt? With Hogan? Who am I—Mary Tyler Moore? What is wrong with me? Must be the heat.

"Come on guys, let's go get our laundry and then meet your new babysitter." I say, even though I know Diane has not technically agreed to it yet, but I am nothing if not an eternal optimist.

Nine

As we walk into Diane's beautiful, freshly decorated house, there is the smell of something healthy and loving simmering on the stove. Her house is spotless; her child's clothes are neat and wrinkle-free. It's also cool. Diane has central air. I can tell just by looking around that in her house everything is always clean: Drips are promptly wiped up, dishes are done after every meal, floors are swept, and the bathroom sink is completely lacking of toothpaste.

In fact, her child looks like he's stepped out of a Tide commercial. There are no holes in the knees of his pants, and his face is completely free from an ice cream beard or a milk mustache.

The kids take her son, Dylan, outside to play and I make a point of telling them to be careful with him.

Diane and I sit down at the table, and she pours us each a glass of sun tea. I want to be Diane when I grow up. She looks so happy. Her teeth are perfectly white. Her hair is gleaming—actually gleaming—and is the perfect shade of blond. Not too blond, but blond enough to be considered beautiful and smart. I run my hands through my curly, tangling-already-from-the-humidity, shit-brown hair and then as I bring my hand down it pauses at the pimple on my chin. Charming.

Diane is talking about the children. How great it will be to have them here. Aren't they sweet and all that? And they are. Through the french doors, the glass ones that are completely lacking of fingerprints that lead out to her spacious deck, I can see that my children are being very good to their new friend. They are building sand castles and being generally well behaved. I try not to look stunned.

We talk for a couple of hours about nothing really. We talk about kids and share birthing stories. For some reason, women who have never met before will sit down and share the most intimate details about birthing their children. She looks shocked when I told her I had a midwife for my last two births and a home birth the last time around. Her husband is an obstetrician, so I suppose this is a foreign concept. She smiles at me. I think she finds me quirky. I have a feeling that Diane doesn't have many quirky friends.

I write down my schedule for her. She seems to be game. We decide on two dollars an hour per kid for my rate. It's a nasty chunk out of my pay, but I can't keep going on like we have been, and it's the cheapest rate I've found so far. The cash in the glove compartment has been hovering around nine hundred dollars, and I know that's largely due to the fact that I don't have to pay a babysitter. Even when I do pay the girls at the restaurant, it's usually only for a few hours until the kids' bedtime. I also know that I will not be able to save as much money once I start paying Diane. But the nights have grown increasingly hot and I cannot, in good conscience, leave them out there anymore. There are just some things you have to do. And this is one of them. Maybe I'll call my mom and tell her that I need money for an apartment. Maybe. But there is still lingering doubt there. Not so much about whether or not she'll give me the money, I am fairly confident she will. But I am not sure I am mentally prepared for the strings that will come with it. Endless guilt, first of all, about how much my life has been thrown off track. Endless discussions about what I should be doing—or worse—what I should have done years ago. Besides, I am viewing this ability of mine to actually employ a babysitter as a step in the right direction. I am progressing. It's a small step, certainly, but it's a step forward, and I don't want to relinquish my pride in that step to anyone. Not even for money.

I chat with Diane and try and act as though I don't really need her to babysit, like I'm just interested in making new friends. I don't want her to know how desperate I am because I am afraid that if she knows that—as well as the fact that we live in the car—she will see us, especially the kids, differently. I feel normal and I don't want Diane, or anyone else for that matter, to know that I'm not.

"How long has your husband been . . . ?" Diane asks.

"Only a couple of months," I say. I know she wants to know if he's dead. I know she thinks he is. I think he is too. I wish he were.

"That must be so hard," she says.

"It is. But, I don't know. You just, kind of, do it."

"Do you have family nearby? Are they helping you?"

"My parents live near Augusta, but . . . well, let's just say that our relationship is strained."

"But it's different now, isn't it?"

"Not really. They never really liked my husband and, well, I've gone back to them for a lot of help over the years, so I just don't want to go back there. Does that make sense?"

"I guess. But still, they have to be there for you, don't they?"

"No. Not really. They have my sisters to take care of. They're both teenagers."

"So, where do you live?"

"Oh, right now I'm staying with my boss in the pub. Just until I can find an apartment." I'm lying again. Why can't I stop? Why can't I just say it out loud? "I'm homeless. We sleep in my car." What is wrong with me?

"Well, that's good, then."

"Yeah. It's fine. I'm too tired right now to be depressed about it. Once we get settled in, I'm sure it will hit me."

"Well, when it does . . . if you want to talk . . ."

"Thanks," I say, trying to perk things up. "That's really nice of you. Now, are you sure you want to take on these little monsters?" Why am I asking this? Do I really want to give her an out?

"Oh, of course. They'll be fine. In fact, why don't they stay over tonight, since you have to work so late?"

"Oh, no. I couldn't let you do that. That's too much."

"No, really. It will be great. Besides you don't want them to interrupt their sleep."

I almost take offense but can't find anything truly offensive in what she said, so I agree.

We call the kids in and explain the plan. They are happy as can be, although Lydia hugs me tight and says how much she'll miss me and kisses me thirty or forty times. Alex is just happy to go off with anyone. I love him for not being afraid of new situations, but at the same time, this fearlessness scares me silly. Frequently he will sit in the cart at the grocery store and just wave and smile to complete strangers. Even though I am standing right over him, I always feel like I have to hold onto him, lest someone comes along and says: "Hey kid, wanna go to China?" Alex wouldn't hesitate, I am sure. He would just say: "Otay!" and kiss me good-bye. And that is just what he does this evening. He sees Dylan heading to the swing set, and he yells "love ya" as he run-waddles and falls continuously away. We really need to have a learn-to-walk session. I laugh, but inside my heart breaks a little. I hope he won't always be so happy to leave me behind.

I am grateful that they will sleep in a real house this night. No worrying about them in the car. Every moment they were out there, all my fears would well up in my stomach and gnaw at me. Would someone walk up to the car and try and take them? Would someone see them and report it to the police? But I knew they were safe—I knew that if anyone tried to take them someone in the kitchen would hear. At least I was almost certain. Stone Harbor is not known for a high crime rate. Like most small towns in New England, most people leave their house doors and car doors unlocked. The worst crimes are usually between people who know each other. An abusive husband or parent. A jealous boyfriend. A poor transient who tries to rob a store, usually with a finger in a pocket trying to make it look like he has a gun. Still, sleeping at the campground was frightening enough. Loud, young men drinking too much and fighting. I had also been reading lately about a rash of murders and assaults on the Appalachian Trail. None had occurred in Maine, as far as I knew, but the idea that even the solitary woods were dangerous was enough to keep me waking up every hour to check on our surroundings.

Fear. My life has become about fear. Feeling it. Living it.

Abating it. I am afraid of the dark. Of what can happen to me and the children in the dark. Of having no money. I am afraid of being a bad mother. Of my car breaking down for good. Of being alone . . . forever. I live with a stomach constantly in knots. My life has become a tunnel, and I am focused on getting through it, but I am afraid of what I will find on the other side. I know what I want to find—at least I think I do—but I fear I have thrown so much bad karma into the world already that I won't get what I want.

But tonight the children, at least, will be safe. They will wake up to the smell of pancakes and sausage cooking in the kitchen. Such a basic thing that I can't provide. It also occurs to me, as I solemnly pull away and head for the bar, that the expense of Diane—as much of a godsend as she is—also means all of our nights will be at the beach from now on. I won't be able to afford the occasional pizza or nights at the campground. This hits me hard, but I also remember that those are nights when the kids will have regular dinners with things like meat. I smile to myself, confident I have done the right thing and notice that the knot in my stomach that has been a constant reminder of my status as "horrible mother" has eased slightly.

The pub is unusually slow for a Friday night, so we start playing Trivial Pursuit for quarters to liven things up. Barb comes into the bar from the kitchen to answer questions and puff on the cigarette she keeps lighting and then putting out. I am up three quarters on everyone when Jay comes in for his shift.

"Not much going on, I'm afraid," I say. "Wanna sit and have a drink instead?"

"Nah," he smiles. I notice how his perfectly straight, perfectly white teeth sparkle against his very tan twenty-eight-year-old skin. "I'll clean glasses." And he hops over the bar, knocking over a couple of glasses and slams into me.

"God, I'm sorry," he says.

"No worries." I wipe the ice that hit me in the chest. I really want to say, "Anytime."

The bar is absolutely barren except for George, a regular who sits at the bar between 10:00 P.M. and 2:00 A.M. every night and drinks vodka martinis without the vermouth and no olive. I tried to explain to him once that this was just vodka, but he said that he prefers the glass. So, a vodka martini it is. If I am feeling especially fruity, I will go through the effort of shaking and straining it. George, however, never believes that I give him his full shot's worth and always tries to count my pour. I quickly learned my lesson with him, and now I go to the other end of the bar to pour his drinks just so he will leave me alone.

Presenting the drink to him, I could have predicted the conversation before it started.

"You shorted me again," he says.

"Oh, shut up will you? I did not, and you know it," I reply.

"You did. I can't even smell the vodka in here."

"You can't smell vodka, George, and if you can, then you have had way too much." I smile my best fake smile and then try to find something—anything—else to do until he requires a refill.

Someone once told me that George was rich, and that he just cashed his checks, wherever they came from, and then drank all day. George told me that he was a lawyer. I kept my smirk to myself. I am so gullible that I will believe almost anything people tell me. This is one of my worst traits—and the fact that I can't judge a person's character worth a damn. I always get people wrong.

Finally, something resembling a crowd starts to come in. A very trendy couple in their mid-forties sits at the bar and spins their tale of antiquing in this, our "cute, little town." Though I'm new to Maine, the tourists are the same ones who visit the quaint Vermont village I grew up in.

When I was twelve, my parents moved us from our huge suburban Maryland home to a then-dilapidated farm in Chelsea, Vermont.

Chelsea was then, and still is, the perfect small Vermont town. Nestled in a valley, the White River Valley, between lush green mountains, Chelsea is somehow found by those tourists who dared drive off the common path to Stowe or Killington.

There were also the leaf-peepers, the tourists who came to Vermont specifically to look at foliage. Those who came to our wee town of Chelsea, population always hovering around 1,100, would pull me and my friends aside while we were walking across the town common to school and ask if they could take a picture of us walking through the leaves. We always obliged the poor tourists and then ridiculed them mercilessly after they had gone.

Although it is a sanctioned pastime in Vermont to make fun of leaf-peepers, just as in Maine it is quite legal to make fun of people who think that all Mainers only eat lobster, it was also a well-honed industry. Vermont—and Maine—I was learning has very few actual industries, so we Vermonters had to take what we could get. Over the years I learned that Vermonters know that playing up to the tourists' imaginations is a good part of what keeps them coming back.

So, into the bar they stagger, tourists looking for a soothing drink after a long day's hike along the sidewalk looking for that perfect little Maine antiquity, or used buoy that they can display in their suburban house. I picture the perfect, little Maine-made Windsor chair lining a wall next to the perfect, little whatever from Milan. Pouring them drinks with cutesy names, like The Rocky Cliff and The Salty Dog Slush—a Salty Dog for lightweights loaded only with top-rail liquor—they easily hand over their money as they ask me for directions to the many microbreweries along the coast or show me the darling little set of teacups made by the "cutest little old man, who has his potter's wheel right there in his house!"

Barb is also at the bar, ranting at George about the lousy tip he left me. Normally, I would be embarrassed by this display, but on this night I am cheering her on in my head. George can take it, I thought, in fact he won't remember it in the morning, and indeed, he flipped Barb the finger and laid a tenner on the bar for me. I change it and split it with Barb, but she flings it back at me and tells me to pour us a couple of screwdrivers.

"Vodka, Barb? You never drink vodka," I tease.

"I drink vodka for breakfast—and I still have to work." Not even I can get away with trying to call her a lightweight—to Barb if it's not whiskey, it's not a real drink.

Hogan's at the bar too. He's there to make sure I "close properly," he says. I think he just wants the company. His girlfriend works at the big credit card company in town, and she works a lot of nights. In fact, from what I hear, the town has never been better off (financially speaking) since the credit card company came to town. Every night, another shift of well-dressed young professionals come in and spend their pay-checks. Before them, the town was floundering, I guess, with fish canneries and a defunct poultry industry.

Jay, who grew up in Stone Harbor, tells me that at one time you couldn't even swim in the bay because there were so many chicken parts floating around in it.

"Gross," I say. I can be so eloquent. "No way."

"Well, it's fine now," he says. "They've cleaned it up since then, but yeah, when I was a kid, there was no way we'd swim in it. That's why a lot of folks who have lived here all their lives still won't go in it."

I had noticed that the water was strangely empty on the days we went down to the beach. Stone Harbor has a small, rocky beach—not really a lie-out-in-the-sun kind of beach, but good for the kids to play in. The real beach is down in Asheville, about halfway between Stone Harbor and Haverhill. The town itself isn't big—a couple of seafood restaurants overlooking the ocean and a craft shop or two—but the beach is brilliant. I first found it on one of our many drives. The kids and I drive all over the place. I love to explore, and it's a great way to kill time. After all we have a mobile home, why not be mobile?

Driving out of Stone Harbor, you lose sight of the ocean for a bit, and you start to drive through woods and hills. It's a pleasant drive and through all the pine trees, somehow you can still vaguely smell the salt air. But then, as you drive through more and more hills, you start to descend, and there you are: Asheville Beach. The length of the beach is not spectacular, but the sand goes into the water forever. You can walk a hundred yards out and still be on the sand, but in the water too. There are great little tide pools, and the kids and I are always collecting sea glass and sand dollars. I hate being homeless, but I love it here. I can't imagine living anywhere else.

I decide to take a break and call my mother. Maybe I can hint enough at needing another five hundred dollars for an apartment. I am actually pretty impressed with my progress. It's only the second week in July and I already have over a thousand dollars saved up. I've been doing really well at the pub. With tips and my paychecks I've made about four hundred dollars a week—a little more than two thousand dollars since I've been here, but I've also spent a lot. Most of it's been on food and I'll admit to going out to eat—so to speak—too often, sometimes as much as two or three times in a week. And I've caved on ice cream many times down at the beach. Gas for the car has also eaten a hole in the budget. I don't drive around too much, but with the exhaust issues, I must be losing gas somewhere.

Still though—a thousand dollars. That's something to be proud of, and I am. Only, with the new expense of Diane as babysitter, I don't know how I'll be able to save much more. I take a deep breath and dial my mom from the payphone in the back of the restaurant.

I start off slow.

"Hi, Mom!"

"Shell, how are you guys?"

"We're good, everything's good here. I love it."

"Oh, that's great," she says. "I'm so happy for you. When are you coming for a visit?"

"Soon. We'll come soon. I have a busy work schedule. But Mom, I'm . . . um . . . having trouble getting an apartment."

"What kind of trouble?"

"Well, what do you think—not enough money trouble?" Don't be snotty, I say to myself. Be cool.

"Well, I can't give you any money, Shell, we just don't have it."

"I know, OK, I'm sorry. But hey, what if—well. What if you watched the kids for me sometimes? I have a babysitter, but I could save a lot more money if you took them sometimes."

"We live forty miles away from Stone Harbor. How can you save money driving here?"

"I don't know, maybe we could stay with you for a bit, or I could just drive it. Dad's had longer commutes than that, right?" I hear a long sigh on the other end of the phone.

"Shell, I told you when you had all those children that I will love them but that you better not count on me to be a full-time babysitter."

"I know, but this is a little different."

"No, Shell, it's not. I will not be one of those grandmothers who takes care of her children's children. They are your children. They are your responsibility."

OK, really, I knew this already. She might as well have been telling me to clean up after my pet gerbil. "Call Tom. They're his children too. Make him babysit for them."

"That's kind of how we got here in the first place, isn't it?" My sarcastic reply flies out of my mouth.

"Look Shell, I just can't. I'll ask your father about the money, but I've given you more than I should have over the last couple of years."

"I know, and I appreciate it. I'm sorry for asking."

"No, no. You were right to ask. But I just can't help you."

"OK. No, I'm fine."

"Look, if you need anything . . ."

"Mom, really, didn't I just ask . . . never mind. I gotta go. Break's over."

"Shell, I love you."

"I love you too, Mom, I'll call you back later." After I'm sure she's hung up, I slam down the phone. Really, Michelle, I think, if you would just tell her the whole truth . . . but God, I wanted her to just read my mind or something. I wanted her to just help no matter how dire the straits are. But I'm not surprised by the exchange. My desire to remain silent—and proud—is not conducive to begging. I hate asking for money. I just hate it. And I hate confrontation. I hate having to explain myself, and I don't want to do it . . . again. I've been apologizing and explaining the choices Tom and I have made for so long that I feel like people—my parents—must just be rolling their eyes and thinking, "Here she goes again." I don't want this, this new life or whatever it is, to be perceived as another one of my grand schemes—like dogsledding, or any of the other "businesses" I have founded over the years. I also know in my heart what I would be thinking if I were my mother. I know what my constant desperation sounds like and maybe I'm trying to give myself the same tough love I'd give me if I were her.

"What?" Barb looks over at me. "Who were you talking to?"

"Just my mother."

"That good, huh?"

"No. It's just. I don't know. I just shouldn't have called, you know?"

"Why, not?"

"Because, I'll just always owe them. It's like a hole I will never get out of. Everything they have ever given me. Every time I've stayed with them. Every dime they ever lent me—it's like a big tally sheet posted somewhere, and they're always keeping track."

"Man, if my parents kept track of everything they ever gave me, hell, I'd never have any money."

"I know, that's what I mean. Why do they always have to

flaunt past failures over my head? Crap. I don't know. I just thought that maybe this time it would be different. That they'd see I was trying to make a new start and that I was doing the right thing for once. Being responsible and all of that."

"Relax, will you? You are the most responsible person I know. And one of the strongest. It takes a lot to accept living in your car and still take care of your kids and reach out for help when you know that your hand might get slapped anyway. It took a lot of guts to call, if you knew they would give you shit about it."

"How did you know I lived in the car?"

"Dahlin," she says with a fake southern accent, "it's obvious. I know you don't have a place to live. If I had a place for the four of you, I'd let you stay there. But you'll be fine. You'll find a place, and you'll do it on your own. You'll raise your kids—and they are great kids—"

"They are, aren't they?" I'm crying now.

"Yes, they are. And you're going to be fine. I know it."

"But what if I'm not? What if I can't do it?" I sniff loudly and am about to wipe my nose on my sleeve when Barb hands me a napkin.

"Then you'll go to your parents' house and sleep on their front porch until they let you in!"

"Yeah. I guess. I don't want you to think my parents are awful. They're not awful. I think they're just sick of my problems and me. I can't really blame them."

"Well, just remember this when your kids are older. Can I ask you a question, though?"

"Sure."

"Do they actually know you're living out of your car?"

"Well, no . . . no, I never . . ."

"Well, then you can't be too hard on them, can you?"

"No, I guess not."

I wipe my eyes and put my apron back on. I smile weakly at Barb.

"Thanks for listening to the rantings of a lunatic."

"No problem. Next time it's your turn."

Ten

With the tourists gone, we can actually have some fun. I have never been able to stay after hours before because of the kids, so this freedom is new to me. Hogan sends George, the last remaining patron, on his way and then locks the door.

Lyle is behind the bar and the rest of us—Hogan, Jay, Barb, Lex, and Rita (Lyle's girlfriend)—are seated at the bar. Lyle serves us drinks, and we keep answering Trivial Pursuit questions. Hogan is cremating us. He knows everything.

"Is this legal?" I ask.

"Of course," Hogan says, hopping up onto the bar. "If the door's locked, it's fine. We're just having a private party."

He leans over the bar, grabs a pint glass, and then pours himself a Guinness, backwards.

"Nice technique," I tease. "Where'd you learn that?"

"I am a man of many talents, I think you'll find," he says. And then he raises his eyebrows and winks at me. If I wasn't so tired I would swoon. I wondered about Hogan once. I thought he was kind of, not cute exactly, but something in his eyes made me think that I could maybe go out with him. But he wears a ring, a big silver one on his left hand. *Must be married*, I thought, and then never considered it again. Instead, I've spent my evenings fantasizing about Jay.

I grab my screwdriver and go and sit at a table—actually, on a table. I swing my legs and sink into the irony of my drink. It is the first peace I have felt in months. The children are fine, happy, and sleeping peacefully at Diane's. I called three times to make sure.

It doesn't take long for the first drink to slide down. I am such a lightweight when it comes to drinking that I'll have to make sure I pace myself or I'll be passed out before I finish my second.

I was never much of a drinker. In high school, I had a lot of friends and was invited to many parties, but I would never go to them. Eventually they stopped asking me. As for pot and other drugs, I hadn't even seen them, much less tried them, until a couple of weeks ago. Lex was sitting out back after one of his shifts, and he was smoking out of a small pipe. A bowl, I am told. I'm such a freak, I didn't even know what to do with it when he offered me some.

"Here have a hit," he said.

"Um . . . nah, I have to go get the kids," I said. Just say no, right? That's what I learned during my Reagan-era school years.

"OK, that's cool," he said. "Have you ever tried it?"

"To be honest, this is the first time I have ever seen it."

"Really? Wow." He was amazed. "Tell you what, the next time you work a night shift, and you don't have to go get your kids, I'll show you if you want. Think about it."

"Yeah, OK," I said, looking at my feet. "Maybe I will." But

I was sure I wouldn't. I had gone twenty-four years without trying a drug. I wasn't going to start now, especially with kids. I must admit, though, it smelled really good. Like a peppery, smoking salad. I remember smelling that smell at a Ziggy Marley concert I went to at Dartmouth College. I had the worst migraine that night, and the smell only enhanced my nausea. I thought that smelling it again would bring that nauseous feeling back, like the time my mom steamed shrimp when I had the flu. I couldn't eat shrimp for years after that. But it didn't. I rather liked the smell.

Lex brings the stuff out again tonight and asks me if I want to try it.

"No kids . . ." he says, trying to tempt me.

"Oh all right, bring it on." He produces a joint and lights it for me. I take it and roll it back and forth between my finger and thumb. I shrug and then, what the hell? I inhale. It burns the back of my throat.

"Is something supposed to happen yet?" I ask. I don't know what I am expecting. Pink elephants and polka dot trees maybe.

"Just relax," Lex replies. "It'll happen."

"OK." And so I wait.

I drag again and then I wait. Nothing. Not even a little woogyness to ease the pain in my back. I give up on trying, eventually, and go back inside. The habit would be too expensive for me to take on anyway, just as I am glad that I never really caught on to smoking cigarettes.

Lyle, tired of trivia, begins the evening's Scrabble tournament. This game is an obsession with him. He posted all our names, as well as the names of interested regulars on the wall. We are to challenge each other, and when we beat an opponent, our name is advanced in the standing. I am really not all that into the game, but it's fun and as long as I stay ahead of George and Hogan in the standings, I'm a happy camper.

"Hey Hogan," I yell. Hogan's sitting at the bar, pretending to be in charge.

"Can I kick your ass in Scrabble, or are you scared?" I'm feeling goofy, but it's not the screwdriver. I am this silly normally, one of the reasons I decided long ago that getting drunk doesn't suit me.

"Oh yeah, Kennedy, bring it on," he says. I'd taken my last name back as soon as I arrived in Stone Harbor. It felt good to be Kennedy again, instead of Mrs. Shepherd. I reach under the bar and grab the Scrabble box. We are not the only pair playing. George, who has since come back (actually, he banged on the door until we let him in because he couldn't find a cab), Jay and Barb are set up at a table. An initiation for Jay, I believe. It's odd. My life is in a shambles, and yet I am having some of the most fun I have ever had in my life.

I am acutely aware that this time in my life is excruciatingly important, but yet, there is part of me that wonders why it's necessary to go through it at all. Why can't comfort at this level be achieved without pain? I have never felt so at home as I do right here, in this little pub, surrounded by people who appreciate me for who I am. They don't care that I tend bar for a living. They don't care that I had three kids before the age of twenty-four. They don't care that I drive a noisy piece of crap. But I care.

Lyle posts another 300-plus Scrabble score, putting my 175 to shame, but I don't care because I still beat Hogan. I get him on *yurt*—he doesn't believe it's a word—but having once considered living in one, I know it is. He challenged it, lost a turn, and that's good for another day or two of sound insulting.

It's 3:00 A.M. and things are starting to wind down. Hogan and the rest are ready to head home. Without the kids around, I feel a little lost. Part of me wants to go grab my sleeping bag and just stretch out on the bar. The warm, smooth mahogany surface couldn't be much less comfortable than the fuzzy carpet in the back of the car. Everyone heads for the door, except for Lyle and Rita, who lock up behind us and then head for his apartment up the backstairs.

A cold rain is coming down and my only protection from it is the doorway overhang. I wave to Hogan and Barb as they head for their cars in the small parking lot across the road. I pretend to look for my keys in my bag as they drive away. I am really looking for the pack of Camel Lights I found behind the bar. I find them and dig for the lighter in my pocket. Hogan has required that all of us bartenders keep both a lighter and a corkscrew on us at all times—it's always good to have a light for a customer, he says. He can be so anal sometimes, but I have to admit that I like his attention to detail.

I sit on the stoop, huge raindrops falling on the back of my head as I try and light the thing in the wind. My body stays dry, but my feet are soaking in the rain. What a pathetic scene—trying to learn to inhale a cigarette while sitting in the rain in front of the bar. This has to be as low as it gets. I would be angry if I wasn't so tired. I rest my chin on my knees.

I flick the cigarette, much like I have seen Lex do, only mine doesn't arc and fall; it goes cattiwampus and sideways, out into a puddle. I pull myself up and drive my car back to the small parking lot beside the bay, noticing that the rain has settled into a cold drizzle. I keep the car running and lay my soaked socks on the floor under the steering wheel so that they can dry from the floor heater. Then I hold my feet up in front of the vents in the dashboard, one at a time, to warm them up. As silly as it would look to someone walking up to the car, it feels extremely good to have the dry heat swirling around my foot.

I lean over the front seat and locate my hiking boots in the back. Slipping them on without socks, I open the car door. I am not the least bit sleepy. Tired, weary even, but not sleepy. I get out of the car and carefully walk around the maze of containers that surround the vehicle. In order to fit into the car to sleep, I stack the Rubbermaid containers around the outside of the car. Matthew calls it the Fortress, and it is—a big, plastic blue fortress, although it reminds me more of an igloo.

I pace the shoreline and rant about the injustice of my life in my head. Pure self-pity, and this time, I have no problem with it. I yell at God for allowing this to happen to innocent children. How can you subject them to such an awful life, and such an awful mother?

The rocks I pitch into the lake are, at first, tiny skipping stones. But as my anger grows, the rocks get bigger and bigger until I am heaving fieldstones into the water and grunting loudly with each one. Each rock represents a person I blame or a judgment I made that I hate.

"That's for marrying the dumb bastard," I yell as the large rock splashes and glugs to the bottom.

"That's for the twit at the welfare office!" I need both arms to push the heavy rock away from my chest. The splash is not satisfactory and so I start grabbing smaller, baseball-sized rocks and imagine pelting the head of Ms. Vande Hei onto the bottom of the lake. I've never pictured myself as particularly homicidal, but it felt extremely good just then.

I spin around to pick up another large rock when a surge of pain shoots through the lower right side of my back. I fall to the ground, in a puddle, of course, and am afraid to move because of the pain, each small twist a surge stabbing through my back.

"Ow! Fuck!" I haven't felt this much pain in one place since the last time I gave birth.

"God, you swear like a sailor," a voice from behind me says. "I should have known."

I whip my head around, too fast, only to find Hogan standing by my car wearing a flannel shirt, jeans and—here's a shocker—Birkenstock sandals. I had only ever seen Hogan wearing a shirt, tie, dark pants, and polished black shoes. His attitude and anal retentiveness had me believing that Birks would be the farthest thing from his wardrobe.

He scratches the top of his balding head with the very short crew cut and walks down toward me. I notice how big a man he is. A peek of the thick hair on his chest makes him look like a bear in the light of the moon, not that I'm looking—besides my back is killing me.

"Camping?" he smiles. What an ass, is all I can think.

"Yeah, something like that," I say. "What are you doing out here at four o'clock in the morning?"

"Well, I was out walking my dog. I live a couple of miles from here, and I heard all this yelling. At first I thought it was someone who needed help, but then I noticed it was just you and your foul mouth. I was going to leave, but then I thought, well, that would be rude."

"You're too kind."

"So, what are you so pissed about?" he looks at me funny. Not like I was the craziest person he had ever seen, which I very well could have been, but more like, concerned.

"Another story for another time," I say, trying to get back in form as my usual jovial self. Never let them see you sweat, or in pain, or in need of anything. Kind of an unspoken motto in my childhood home.

"Where is this alleged dog of yours?"

"Somewhere." He turned his head and yelled, "Astro!"

"You named your dog Astro? You have got to be kidding me."

"Shut up, it's a great name."

"OK, Mr. Spacely, whatever you say." I can't help but laugh, and suddenly I am laughing my ass off—this seems so bizarrely funny to me, to be talking with a guy, who named his dog Astro, at four o'clock in the morning. It feels good, though, to be making fun of somebody instead of wallowing in self-pity.

"Hey, I thought you lived out of town a ways. What are you doing down here?"

"I don't know," he says. "Sometimes I just take off with Astro and come down here. I can't always take being in the house."

"Trouble in paradise?" I joke. He and his girlfriend, Jane, always seem so happy when they're in the pub together. Just the other day I was sitting at the bar with her. I was going through the classifieds, looking for an apartment, as usual, and she was rattling on about how she and Hogan met. I don't remember much of it, but I did recall her saying something about how they were fated to be together because they had the same initials—JMH.

"It's hardly paradise," he says. "I've been sleeping on the couch for months. Why do you think I work so many nights? Besides, I think she's seeing someone at the bank."

"Really?" I am stunned by this information. "You two seem to get along so well."

"Yeah, well, I don't know. Who knows? My first wife cheated on me, so I guess I kind of expect it."

"You've been married?" More information that I'm not prepared for.

"Yeah. Technically, I still am. I haven't seen her in five or six years, since I left for Ireland, and I never got around to getting a divorce. It's no big deal though, I really don't want to get married again anyway."

"I hear that," I say, trying to contribute in some way to the conversation.

"And it gives me a good excuse to avoid marrying Jane."

"Well, that doesn't sound very nice." I smile, though, so he knows I'm teasing him.

"You know, I ought to go. I should get some sleep—I have to open tomorrow, I mean, later. Do we need to talk about this?" He asks pointing to the car and all of my things stacked up around it. "Do you need anything?"

I just shake my head and look at the ground. While I stare at my feet, a huge mouth, full of slobber that seems to belong to a dog, comes up under my face. Astro. I ruffle the fluff of white fur around his ears and lean my head on his forehead.

"Well, I guess we'll head out then," Hogan says. "Are you sure there isn't anything we can do for you?"

"Not unless you have an extra house on you." I'm only half-joking.

"Not today, but I will keep a lookout for you," he says. "You know though, there are some weekly motels around, why not check one of those out?"

"Because then I'd waste all the money I earn on a place where I don't want to live. If I can just hold out a little longer, I'll be able to afford a decent apartment."

"Fair enough," he says. And he walks away. That glimmer about Hogan comes back. What would he possibly see in me when he has a smart, beautiful girlfriend already? I'm not disappointed, exactly, to hear they're having trouble, but why? What could I possibly want from him? I'm sure they'll work it out. Besides, I'm concentrating on a fantasy life with Jay. And it's not like there's much of a singles market for a twenty-four-year-old homeless woman with three children. So, fantasy is about all I have left in that department—probably a good thing, considering that anything else gets me pregnant. I close my eyes, tired from gazing at the lights on the lakefront houses.

I stretch out in the back of the car—well, as much as one can possibly stretch out in a car—and am by myself for the first time in months. Am I selfish? Maybe I am being too hard on Tom. But if that's true, then where is he? I called him about a week after we got here and told him where I work. Why hasn't he come yet? Is this the way it's supposed to end? Tom was my soul mate. At least, I tried to make him that way. He has been my only friend for the last seven years. I can't believe we're just over. It's weird to think about the choices you make that bring you to your life as it is. Every choice bringing you down a different path. Or is it fate? I guess that's the eternal question, isn't it? What is it about me that makes me think that I am such a special person, such a great person, that I could do all this stuff by myself? That I don't need a husband or a man or whatever, when it is quite I obvious that I do. I can't do things alone—if I could, I wouldn't be living in a car, now would I?

4:35 A.M. That's the time my Indiglo watch illuminates back at me. What day is it? I can't remember. A Tuesday maybe? My heart is pounding. I'm sweating. My mind is turning over and over. My head is pounding, too. A sharp stabbing pain in the base of my brain circulates around my entire head. I drank too much. Or maybe it was that joint I tried. Maybe it did have an effect. I open my eyes and try and focus on a street light not far from here. The light hurts my eyes. I close them again and try to be still so the pounding will stop.

I lie back down. I wish I could just die. Just float away. No money to worry about. No job. No car. No crappy ex-husbands. Just die. It wouldn't be hard, would it? To just let it all go.

Shit, my head hurts.

Wouldn't it be easier if I was just gone? I could make out a will. Leave the kids to my parents. Surely, with me gone, they'd take them on. It's just me they can't deal with. I could wait until the kids go to Diane's and drive off a bridge. What would the kids think if I died? Would their lives be better? They would have to be, wouldn't they?

But God, I would miss them. I would miss Alex's sly little smile. Matthew's explanation for why everything in the world works. Lydia dancing along the rocks at the beach. I wouldn't get to see them graduate from high school, or have families, or explore careers. I wouldn't get to see what they will be when they grow up.

A lump is hardening in my throat. Tears filling my eyes. I'm selfish. I know I am. I don't want to die because I don't want to not be a part of their lives. Maybe they would be better off without me. Maybe. Maybe I'm the worst mother in the whole world, but my heart aches more than my head at the thought of not being with them for even one day.

It's 5:00 A.M. I have to pick up the kids in two hours. Would you just go to sleep?

I sleep for about two hours and then head up the road toward Diane's house. I stop at the mini-mart and get coffee and a newspaper, in the vain hopes that someone will only want two hundred dollars for a great apartment. The problem, of course, is that with the credit-card company in town now, the economy is growing, and apartments have become impossible to find. And the people I am competing with have money to spend. I've been outbid twice. Another time a guy offered to pay the full year's rent in advance while I could only offer the first month's rent and half the security deposit.

I sit in the car and glance at the front page. Christ. I can't believe it. It's my birthday, July 12th. I am a quarter of a century old today. Happy Birthday. Immediately though, my mood improves. There is just something about your birthday that makes you feel special. I get the kids, and we go to the beach. We are going to have fun. I raid the apartment stash—very irresponsible, I know—and buy the kids each a new toy for the sand.

We have a late lunch/early dinner at the pub. Hogan serves us. I tell him it's my birthday. I tell everyone I know. I still do this. I'm like a child about my birthday. People I wait on who are in the restaurant, Lyle, Rita, Barb. I tell them all. I eat a beautiful salad Barb has created called the mandarin beef salad. It's strips of steak on a bed of mesclun with mandarin oranges and a vinaigrette. It's perfect. The kids have peanut butter and fluff. I tell them to order anything they want, and that's what they pick. Savages!

A package is at the bar waiting for me.

"You shouldn't have," I say to Hogan.

"I didn't," he says, handing me a knife so that I can cut the tape on the box. I open the card. It's from my parents. They've sent me cash—one hundred dollars. I smile as I slip the crisp bill into my pocket. I dig around in the box and pull out wind chimes. I'm trying to understand this gift. Is it a housewarming gift for when I get a house? Is it inspiration? Or is it a new rearview mirror ornament? Puzzled, I slip them back into the box. I put my hand in my pocket and finger the one-hundred-dollar bill. It's amazing how when I was a kid a hundred dollars would have seemed like a million. How quickly it goes now. A hundred dollars could be twenty or even one. Between gas and food and a campsite—I could make it disappear in a flash. But I try not to think about that now. I just want to enjoy owning it for a little while. I make a mental note to call my parents and have a short, grateful conversation with them. Any more than that and I'll just get hurt. Especially if I have to hear again how my younger sisters got yet another car bought for them. But I won't be hostile. I'm sending only good karma out into the air, in the vain hope that maybe some of it will come back to me someday.

Hogan plays the Beatles' "Happy Birthday" song on the stereo behind the bar for me. All of a sudden, I'm having a party. There's a message on the bar from my mother telling me to look out for her gift. I'm very grateful for it, but not in the mood to call her and thank her just yet. I'll save that for to-morrow. Rita, who owns a cute little jewelry shop on a side street, produces a beautiful pair of earrings for me. People buy me drinks. I start with sodas and virgin mai tais. Barb takes the kids to the kitchen, and they make me a cake. It is without a doubt the best birthday I've ever had, and it's the standard I will hold all subsequent birthdays to. The kids are starting to tire just as the trio of musicians, who are scheduled to play, shows up. Matthew is fascinated with their gear and is mes-merized by the man with a violin.

We sit and laugh, and the kids run around, except for Alex, who is permanently fixed to my lap. Just the other day, we had a meeting upstairs in the server station, a little room where we keep coffee, extra silverware, and china just off the dining room. It was my day off, but it was a mandatory meeting, so I told Hogan that if he wanted me to come, he would have to let me bring the kids because I hadn't asked Diane to babysit for me. Of course, he agreed. Matt and Lyd sat down on the floor and were mostly quiet. Alex stood by me against a wall. He was pretty shy. Hogan came into the room and sat down on a bench. Alex walked right across the room and sat down on the bench next to Hogan. He leaned on him, cuddling up under his arm. I was absolutely mystified. And Hogan surprised me too. He put his arm around Alex and just sat there with him, hugging him, leading the meeting.

Lydia and Alex, now in complete sugar shock, need to go to bed. Lyle's niece, who is staying with him for a few weeks, offers to take them upstairs to watch TV. I accept and give her twenty dollars—in my birthday enthusiasm, all of a sudden money has become no object.

After letting Matt stay up a while longer to listen to the musicians, things start to get loud in the bar, so I send him upstairs too. He replies with a perfectly pitched, "Aw, Mom," that makes everyone in the bar say, "Aw, Mom."

"Shut up all of you! I'm his mother, and he goes to bed." I smile at Matt and he half-smiles, half-mopes as he slowly ascends the stairs, soaking up the attention.

"Good night, Matt," they all yell. Matt waves, gives me one last glance, and then sulks away.

"You mean mommy," Barb says.

"Yup, that's me. I'm the meanest."

I bid Matthew a final farewell and then sit up at the bar, ready for my first real drink of the evening. I only drink for taste, so I ask Jay—who is now behind the bar, having relieved Hogan of his duties—to make me a frozen mudslide. They are dessert in a glass. And Jay puts just the right amount of whipped cream and a little drizzle of Kahlua on top.

I hold my drink and spin around to see the trio when Hogan comes up next to me.

"Thanks for the impromptu party," I say.

"I didn't do anything," he says. "They all just showed up—it is a bar you know."

"I know," I smile. He smiles too. I don't know if I have ever seen him really smile. I've seen him smirk plenty of times, but never smile. And truth be told, I am just as intimidated by him as anyone else.

He puts his arm around me.

"You know," he says, looking down at me with a strange, kind look in his eyes, "in three years, you are the only person who has ever made me consider leaving my girlfriend."

"Oh hah!" I say. "Those Irish girls that were in here the other night got you going pretty well!" Joking is the best way for me to deal with any shock. And I am shocked.

I am stunned, in fact. What an odd thing to say. Does he mean it? There's no way he meant it. He's too old for me anyway. He must be nearly forty. He's been drinking—that must be it.

Still though . . . it makes me wonder.

Eleven

Hogan and I have started to play a little head game in the pub. It's called the "marriage sucks, let's go down in the basement and do it" game. When it's slow, we sit and talk and flirt shamelessly. I don't know why I participate exactly. I have absolutely no interest in Hogan at all—physically anyway. But he's really nice under his gruff façade, which I have since informed him is a way of covering up his deep, sensitive side.

"Bullshit," he says.

"No, I'm serious," I say. "You act like a big bully on the outside so that people will have to respect you, but inside, you're a softy. I've witnessed it."

"What have you witnessed?"

"Your soft side. That time I had to bring the kids to the meeting? I could see it. Alex walked right up to you. If you were really mean, you would have sent him back to me, but you didn't, you picked him up and sat him on the bench beside you."

"So?"

"So, then I knew that you have a heart lurking underneath all that hair somewhere."

During one of our more rabid flirtations I told Hogan I'd never go out with a guy with a really hairy chest. He took this moment to unbutton one or two buttons of his shirt and show me his very hairy chest. A perfect reason, I said, to keep pursuing Jay.

"I think you should just come down to the basement with me and see what it's really like," he said.

"All right, I'm game," I said, knowing he didn't mean it. "Let's go."

I think I made him blush because he got up to clean off some tables.

I sit at the bar and go through the classifieds some more. The same old apartments, or at least, the same landlords with the same buildings. I must know them all by now. The kids and I have been to every apartment building within a ten-mile radius of this town, which isn't saying a lot because most of the apartments are downtown within a ten-block radius of the pub.

I spot an ad that says it takes Section 8 renters.

"What's a Section 8 renter?" I ask Hogan who is now polishing the brass rails along the bar.

"It's government-assisted housing," he says. "In most places, it's pretty bad."

"Yeah, but how bad could it be here?"

"You never know," he says. "But it's probably worth checking out."

"I probably won't qualify. I didn't qualify for food stamps."

"You applied for food stamps?" He says this in a real snotty tone.

"Don't get all uppity on me, Hogan. I thought it would help and besides, like I said, I didn't qualify."

"I'm sorry, you're right, it's just I get so pissed off at those people sometimes."

"What people?"

"The people on food stamps. Here I am in the checkout line trying to make my house payments and Jane's car payment and whatever, so I have to eat like mac and cheese out of the box and the people in front of me have junk food piled to the rafters and they pay with food stamps."

"I'm sure not everyone is like that," I say. "There is always someone who'd rather buy Ding Dongs than fruit. Hey, I would."

"Yeah, but you wouldn't do it," he says.

"Well, I agree that they should make it so you have to buy a certain amount of nutritious food with them, but at the same time, then you are allowing the government to dictate what you can eat."

"Yeah, but if they're paying for it . . ."

"Oh, whatever," I say, physically exasperated by this conversation. "I have to pay cash, so what does it matter to me anyway? Give me the phone, I'm going to call the bitch at the food-stamp place about this housing."

I can't get any more information about the program without making an appointment to come in and apply for it. I was hoping they could tell me whether or not I had a chance first, but the receptionist just says, "Every case is different."

I make my appointment for the next morning and call on a few other interesting apartments. They are all rented. I give one man the number of the pub because he thinks someone might be leaving at the end of the month.

"Hey," Hogan says, seeing the frustration mounting. "Why don't you cut out early and go hang with your kids? Things look like they'll be slow tonight anyway, and Jay will be in soon."

Normally, I don't like being cut early because I don't like to lose any potential money, but it's a hot and sticky Tuesday night and if I don't make anything, I'll have to cut into the apartment stash to pay Diane.

"Yeah, all right," I say. "Are you sure?"

"Sure I'm sure," he says. "We'll do the basement tomorrow."

"Oh God, get a life," I say.

"I'm trying," he says, as I push out the front door.

Matt, Lydia, and Dylan are running around a small plastic wading pool when I get to Diane's. Alex is in the pool, splashing and laughing. They look so cute, I think. How can I possibly deserve such adorable children? They run up to me, soaking wet, their legs covered in grass, and hug me.

"Hey guys," I say. "I got out early today."

"Yea!" they yell. How can they be happy to see me? Me being early just means a night in the car, but they are happy anyway, and I am happy for it. I walk over and give Alex a quick kiss and then go up to Diane on the deck. She's knitting something and watching the kids from her lawn chair.

"Hi," she says. "They let you out early today."

"Yeah, it was slow. How is everybody?"

"Good. Matt and Lyd had a bit of an incident over a board game, but I separated them for a bit and now they seem fine."

"That's cool," I say. "Did Lydia get mad that she wasn't winning again?"

"How did you know?"

"She hates to lose. Last time we played Candy Land, she threw the board across the room."

"That's exactly what she did this time!" Diane laughs.

"I don't know how to get it through to her that it's just Candy Land for chrissakes!" I say. Diane winces a little at my swearing. I've learned to keep it in check around her. She's a lot of fun to talk to, but I do tend to get in the habit of swearing too much at the restaurant. Every other word in the kitchen is fuck and I have to watch myself back out in the real world.

"Anyway," she says. "How is that Hogan fellow?" Diane's so funny, calling him a fellow. It's a little like talking to my grandmother sometimes. I tell her about the incident on my birthday, and she says he sounds cute.

I tell her Hogan is definitely not cute, but handsome in a rugged kind of way.

"Well, OK, maybe cute's the wrong word," she says. "But doesn't he have a girlfriend?"

"Yeah, but it doesn't sound like it's working out."

"Hmmm . . . that's promising . . ." she says. "It might be too soon though, for you, I mean."

"Oh definitely," I say. "I don't even want to think about dating or anything." I'm a little overly emphatic about this. "It's just fun to think that somebody could be interested in me, you know? It's been a long time since anyone liked me that way."

"Sure, sure," she says. "I know exactly what you mean. I mean I love David and we're happy and all, but sometimes you just kind of miss that . . . thrill . . . of meeting someone for the first time."

"You know, Tom was the first guy I was ever serious about, and I married him so young. I've never dated as a grown-up."

"Me too," she says. "I mean, David and I married while he was in med school, but we've been together since our junior year of high school."

"It's just weird to think that I might go out with someone else someday—or anything else," I say, trying to tread lightly on the subject of sex. If Diane winced at my swearing, I didn't know how far I could take that subject.

"Oh, I know," she says, surprising me, "I can't imagine what it would be like to sleep with anyone besides David. Not that I haven't tried to picture it!"

We laugh, and then the kids run up and whine about how hungry they are.

"Why don't we grill some hot dogs and hamburgers for them?" Diane offers. "David won't be home until late, and Dylan and I were planning on the kids staying anyway."

"No, we couldn't."

"Oh, you know you want to," she says, uncorking a bottle of white zinfandel. "Besides, I want to drink this and I don't like the thought of drinking alone, it makes me feel like Joan Crawford."

"All right," I say, "if you're sure. But let me cook—you've had the kids all day in this heat and the little bit of work I did on my shift was easy."

"Sounds good to me," she says, putting her feet up on the deck rail. "Now go off and play, you guys. We'll call you when dinner is ready."

"And stop leaving poor Alex alone in the pool!" I call after them. I can see him and know he's fine, but he looks so lonely out there by himself.

"OK," they whine, but they go off to play.

"Wow," Diane says watching the kids run around. "I don't know how you do it."

"Do what?" I ask, patting the ground beef into something resembling a hamburger. It's a good thing I don't work in the kitchen—Barb would hate me.

"How you keep them so happy all by yourself? Don't they miss him?"

"Yeah, we talk about him sometimes. He wasn't around a lot though, and things have been really hard these last couple of years, so I guess they're kind of used to it. It's got to be better than all the yelling and screaming we used to do."

"How can it be better?" Diane sounds shocked by my nonchalant response and I realize I've kind of put my foot in it. I forgot that she thinks—at least I think she thinks—I'm a widow. I decide to try and clear it up carefully.

"Well, I haven't talked to him since we moved here, but I'm sure they'll see him sometime, if they want to."

"Oh!" she says, immediately catching on. "Oh. That's good then."

"Yeah. All right," I say trying to change the subject, "these are all made up. How do I turn on your grill?"

Diane gets up and turns on her gas grill. Cool, I think, a grill that makes fire without pinecones and dry leaves.

We all eat on the deck, picnic-style. A little heady from the wine and the heat, I down two big glasses of water. I clean up, while Diane gets the kids changed into dry clothes. I feel like things are a little uncomfortable between Diane and me, but I could be imagining it. She seems a little awkward. Maybe she's embarrassed. I am, but we solidify my schedule for the next week, and I give her a hug before we head out to the car.

"Thanks for dinner," I say. "And for letting me talk."

"Anytime." She smiles. "And keep me informed about that Hogan fellow."

I'm still turning the conversation over in my head when we

pull up to the pub. Lyle is having a local Irish band play and I think the kids will get a kick out of it. Besides, I really don't want to do the bedtime routine right now. We could use some culture. Culture is definitely something that's been lacking in our lives.

We hop up on the bar stools nearest to the service bar so I can at least talk to people I know while we're here.

"I thought you said it would be slow tonight." I say to Hogan as he pours the requisite three Shirley Temples.

"It will be. I don't know why he's having them play on a Tuesday," he says. "I think he's trying to draw people in, but it just seems more expensive to me."

"Well, who knows? We'll enjoy it though, right guys?" The kids bob their heads up and down as they stuff the cherries into their mouths.

"Hey, I was thinking," Hogan says, leaning on his elbows and talking directly to the kids, "your mom has an appointment tomorrow morning, and I thought we could go to the movies."

"Yeah!" they all yell, turning the heads of the people at the two tables that are actually taken. "Can we, Mom? Can we?"

"Oh, I don't know, guys," I say. "Hogan, that's too much. Do you know what it's like to take these guys anywhere?"

"Oh, Kennedy, it's just a movie. They have a ten A.M. showing in the summer. It's a Disney movie. Besides, I've been dying to see it."

"Please, Mom? Please?" And just how am I supposed to say no to this? At the same time I am wondering if Hogan is a child molester or something. Why would he offer to do this? Hogan looks right through me.

"Come on, Kennedy, it won't be so bad. I want to see the

movie, but I'd look stupid going in there by myself, wouldn't I? And you can go to your appointment alone."

"Oh, all right. But you guys better be good."

"We will," Matt and Lyd promise.

"Uh huh, sure," I say. "How about you, Al? Wanna go to a movie tomorrow?"

He nods his head and smiles as if he goes to movies everyday.

"All right, you win, Hogan. I'll meet you at the theater?"

"Sure," he says, and he winks at the kids. They love him now. My own heart lurches, but I refuse to recognize it as anything important.

We listen to the music for a while. Matthew is mesmerized by a college kid playing the violin. "It's a fiddle, Mom," he says. And Lydia dances around the room. Al dances too, but it's more of an in-one-place baby waddle.

"This is your last chance to bail out," I call to Hogan as I try and gather the kids to leave. Lydia decides to throw a tantrum—one I am sure will cure Hogan of his desire to watch them tomorrow—and I have to put Alex down on the floor, pick her up off the floor and physically stand her up and then pick Al up again. I hold Lydia by the hand and half pull, half drag the now wailing child out of the restaurant.

"See you in the morning," Hogan calls.

"You're insane," I call back and push through the door before he can reply.

Back at the campground, I search through my backpack and assemble the appropriate papers for my encounter with the housing services department while the kids sweat themselves to sleep. I am nervous. I want this to go right, but something in my gut tells me it won't. Something tells me I'll need to file a million forms and will have to wait forever for an answer. I saw this documentary on public television once about a woman trying to get off welfare, and it took her a year to get public housing. She and her kids had to live in these awful temporary shelters until then. They were filled with drug addicts and gang members and families with poor little kids. The woman said that dirty diapers and needles were everywhere. God, at least we don't live in a city. At least I have the car. It might be awful to live in it, but it's still our own private space.

We wake up early, and the kids are jabbering about the movie from the second they wake up. They haven't even seen it yet, and they sound like they know all about it.

"The commercials, Mom," they say. "We saw them at Diane's."

"Oh, right," I say. "Come on, get your teeth brushed."

"Mom," Lydia says. "We haven't eaten breakfast yet. We shouldn't brush our teeth until after we eat."

"Well, this morning you're gonna, little miss," I say. "At least it will keep your breath from being stinky!"

Matt laughs. Lydia flicks her wet toothbrush at him.

"Mom, Lydia hit me with water."

"It's just water, Matt, stop whining," I say. "Lydia, just brush your teeth."

Meanwhile, Alex is trying to run and I am trying to dry him off from his shower. He's getting used to the shower. Before he gets in, I have to put my hand over the nozzle to make it more "wike wain." I gradually take my hand off, and he just stands there, letting it pour over him. I take him to the side and soap him up and then he goes back under on his own. I'm grateful for this new skill—showering with him was getting too hard. At the same time, I still can't have a shower to myself. I make the kids stand right along the dressing room wall while I shower so I can keep an eye on them. We have a quick break-fast of Nutri-Grain bars and juice. I figure they'll eat a ton of popcorn and candy—for lunch no less—at the theater.

We arrange the car back to car mode, and I see Hogan waiting out front when I pull up to the theater.

"Hey guys," he says. "Are you ready?"

"Here you go," I hand him forty dollars. Precisely why we never go to the movies. It's a costly excursion, but I certainly don't expect him to pay. He hands it back.

"It's on me."

"No, the kids are too expensive, and they'll want to eat everything," I say.

"It's better than spending it on Jane," he says, and then the kids take him by the hands—even Alex—and pull him into the theater.

"I'll meet you at the pub in a couple of hours?" I call. He nods, and then is sucked up by my children into the dark cool of the theater, and I am left out on the sidewalk wondering what the hell he meant by that.

I climb back into the car and thread my way through the cars from New York and Massachusetts back to the Job Center. Why do they give it a name like the Job Center? It's so deceiving, so optimistic. They should just call it what it is—the welfare office. Don't try and dress it up with hope and optimism.

I walk in, decidedly less optimistic than the first time I was here. Nothing has changed. The carpet is filthy, the applicants are filthy, and the smell has grown more stale with the warmer weather. I don't want to be here. But I walk up to the desk and ask for the application for subsidized housing.

I fill it out, turn it in, and wait my turn.

A different voice calls my name this time. I don't know why

I expected it to be Ms. Vande Hei again. This woman is young and chipper, obviously new to social work, I thought.

We go through the application a line at a time. She enters in all of my information and then discovers I have been here once before.

"Oh, good," she says, "We won't have to reenter everything." Glad I could make your life easier, I think.

"Let's see, last time you applied for food stamps, yes?"

"Uh huh."

"And you didn't qualify?"

"Yes," I say, trying to be my ever-friendly and cheerful self.

"Now you'd like housing assistance?"

"Yes?" This comes out like a question. "Yes." I say again, trying to be more confident.

"Where are you staying now?"

"With friends," I say. I have to say this. I practiced saying this. I don't want them to have any reason to take the kids away. I'm not sure if they would, but I don't want to give them any reason at all.

"And that's not working out?" I want to say, "Well, duh . . ."

"It's just stressful, that's all," I say. "I have some money saved, but I need the rest of a security deposit. I just need help getting into an apartment. I don't need help with the rent."

"I see," she says. "And your ex-husband? How much does he pay in child support?"

"Well, he's not my ex, yet, and I don't know exactly where he is."

"This would be a lot easier if you could find out."

"Why?" I'm confused.

"Because then we could either help you through the divorce process, and you could get child support, or you could file a paper claiming abandonment."

"Oh."

"I don't know," she says. "Let me see. Can you be reached at this number during the day?"

"Yes."

"Let me sort out what we need from you and I'll call you, OK?" She stands up and reaches for my hand.

"OK." I get up quickly and shake her hand.

"You can find your way back out?"

"Yeah," I say.

"Great, I'll call you in a couple of days."

In a couple of days I'll find out that they lost my application and I'll have to apply all over again. I don't.

My appointment lasted all of a half hour, and I now have an hour and a half to kill before I meet Hogan and the kids. I sit in the car and count my money again. I also pull the money out of my front pocket and count that. It's been almost a month since the kids started going to Diane's and I've had to tap into the box several times to pay her, meaning my "balance," if you can call it that, hovers around eleven hundred dollars. It's gone up a few times, but then I have to use it again to pay her. I hate to think it, but I really did save more money when they slept in the car. Don't even think it, I say to myself. They're better off going to Diane's. Maybe Lyle would promote me to bartender. That way I would make at least five dollars an hour plus tips, rather than being a waitress who knows how to bartend. I don't know why bartenders make more. Waitressing is definitely harder, but there it is. I decide to ask Hogan about it first, before asking Lyle.

I walk around town for a while and then head up to the pub. Jay gives me a Diet Coke while I wait for my gang. I just sit and enjoy the air-conditioned air and the view of Jay cleaning up the bar. I never realized how much I enjoyed quiet before. I love to just sit and not have to do anything. Even when the kids are sleeping, there is always a kind of noise. I think it's mostly in my head, but it's just the constant worrying about them and watching over them. Right now, they are with Hogan and for some reason I feel completely comfortable with that. I know they are safe, and I can enjoy this quiet. I never knew this kind of peace when Tom had the kids. Even if he took them into the yard while I cleaned the house, I was always worried that something would happen to them. I don't have that gnawing feeling now and I'm surprised by its absense.

An hour and three pint-size Diet Cokes later, the happy foursome skip through the door.

"Hi, guys." I wave. "How was it?"

"It was awesome," Matt says.

"Yeah, it was great," Lydia says, "but Alex got scared."

Hogan walks in, carrying Alex and his diaper bag.

"He didn't get too scared, did you, Bud? It was just a little loud in there." Alex nods his head and covers his ears. "Too woud," he says.

"He was OK after a while. It just took some getting used to."

"Where did you guys sit?"

"Right up front," Matt says. "Everything was huge!"

"Yup, right up front," Hogan says, massaging his neck.

"Sorry, I should have warned you." I smile. Hogan looks almost cute, rubbing his neck and carrying a diaper bag.

"No worries," he says. "It was fun. Now, I promised you guys lunch, so what do you want?"

"Lunch—didn't you have popcorn for lunch?" I ask, figuring they had eaten their fill of junk food.

"Mom," Lydia says, "popcorn doesn't fill you up."

"Oh, sorry," I say.

Hogan fills out an order for three peanut butter and fluff sandwiches.

"So," he says, "how was your appointment?"

"Hideous. I don't want to talk about it."

"That good, huh?"

"No, they are awful people over there. Trying to get assistance is a part-time job in itself. If I wanted to spend that much time doing that crap I'd just get a second job."

"Something will turn up."

"Yeah, sure." I can feel a lump forming in my throat and I don't want to cry, certainly not in front of the kids and Hogan of all people. "Thanks for taking them out. It really was above and beyond."

"It was nothing, but I don't know how you do it all the time."

"Me either." I pick at Lydia's fruit salad and wait for them to finish so I can take them to Diane's before looking at another round of apartments and then going back to work.

Twelve

It is freezing, flipping cold. It is mid-August and very early in the morning. Light just breaking over the forest we are parked under. I forgot that summer in New England was a Tuesday—an old joke my father used to tell. Christ, it's cold. Lydia's birthday passed at the end of July like just another day. Well, not completely. Hogan came through once again, and we had a small party for her in the pub. The night before, he suggested we take a break together and went walking downtown to look for presents for her.

"I don't know, Kennedy, what does a four-year-old girl like?" he asked, fingering the cloth of a pretty batik dress at an imports shop.

"Oh, you don't have to get her anything. I'm just glad to have the company," I said.

"No, no. I want to get her something. I know. She told me one day she wants a hat like the girl in the Alaska movie—what kind of hat is that?"

"Um . . . if I recall it's like a floppy, taupe rain hat."

"What's taupe?"

"Like beige."

"Oh. OK—how about this?" He modeled a hat matching my description and twirled for me.

"Large Irish men with goatees should not model children's hats," I laughed. "But I think it's perfect—for her."

"Great, I'll get this. And the dress."

"Hogan, don't. It's too much."

"Shut up, I want to."

I shrugged and picked out a variety of musical instruments I knew I'd regret buying later. It seemed so strange wandering the stores with Hogan, yet oddly comfortable. As if we did it all of the time. It felt nice to just be with someone who knew all my circumstances and still liked me in spite of them. There was really nothing sexual about it—no accidentally touching each other or anything. Just comfortable.

The kids are plenty warm, bundled in their comforters, but I am tossing, turning, and rubbing my hands and feet in the front seat. I am so cold that my teeth actually chatter against each other involuntarily. I don't want to run the car because I am very low on gas and so I climb into the backseat and huddle under the covers with the kids. God, did I really own a dogsled team and like winter at one point? I can't believe I was that insane.

It's extremely tight. I have to scrunch Alex in next to me like a wee baby and then turn Matt and Lydia on their sides— each facing a wheel hub. I can't really sleep, but at least I am warm . . . although the tip of my nose is cold.

"I will end this today," I say out loud, although the kids are still sleeping.

I really thought we could hold out until I saved a few more hundred dollars, but it's not working. Someone is going to have to rent us an apartment, or I'll have to go to one of those weekly motels. They dot the coast. Little clusters of cabins. But I didn't want to live in one. I read in the newspaper that I could get one fairly cheap during the off-season, for maybe a hundred dollars a week. OK, that seems like a good deal, but if I spend that much on a little cabin, between babysitting and food and everything, that leaves us next to nothing to get an apartment with. And those cabins go up to about five hundred dollars a week in the summer for the tourists. Which means that next summer I am right back where I started this year. No way. It has to be an apartment.

I still have my eleven hundred dollars stashed in the glove box, plus about forty dollars in ones in my jacket pocket. I need fifteen hundred dollars to get an apartment. That's just the apartment—no furnishings, no food. But it would be a place to live. A home.

It's a day off. A rare Saturday—day and night—to myself, to ourselves. There is part of me that hates the idea of taking a day off, but the mom in me is happy to have a day with the kids—not to mention the time to find an apartment and maybe do laundry. It seems a pity to waste such a lovely day off doing errands and chores, but I can't think of any activity that could truly make a day off worthwhile.

I consider making a fire for all of us to warm up by, but settle for starting up the car while we get dressed, because I don't want to smell like campfire while we're looking for a place to live.

To celebrate my newfound resolve, I take the kids to the town diner for breakfast, the Hometown Café. Everything is trimmed with chrome. The tables and the counter are all

Formica, and trimmed with chrome; the dishes all melamine. Alex is enamored with the little jukeboxes at each table and even though it's only 8:30 in the morning, I let Matthew put a quarter in and let Lydia pick the song. Alex is an absolute riot, bopping his head to "Blue Suede Shoes," while waiting for his pancakes. A couple of the patrons look annoyed by our selection so early, but hey—if they didn't want us to play the jukeboxes . . .

Wow. I feel normal. I feel like a normal person, sitting here, waiting for someone else to bring us our food. I wish I could afford it more often.

The kids are well behaved, and this is not the first time I receive compliments on their good manners in public, but the one thing they are not is tidy eaters. They are slobs in fact. They never act like animals, but there is always an accidental knocking over of a milk glass—or syrup overflowing from a plate and landing on a seat. Usually, the culprit chooses to sweeten his french toast further while I am under the table looking for a dropped fork. But I always leave an extra large tip because I feel so sorry for the person who has to clean up after us, even if the service isn't great. I'd go and apologize in person, but I don't want to have to look the person in the face.

I left my paycheck behind the bar the night before, and so we walk up the hill to O'Hara's. The pub itself won't be open yet, but someone, either Hogan or Barb, will be there. We stop in a couple of shops along the way. I love some of the gift shops in Stone Harbor. But I can always tell that shopkeepers are wary of my tribe and me before we enter. So I have come up with the hands-in-pockets rule. When we go into a shop, I announce that everyone must put their hands in their pockets. This usually gets me a big smile from the person behind the counter.

"But I don't have any pockets," Lydia says with a smile.

"Then put them behind your back," I say.

Meanwhile, Matt has chosen to show off his cleverness by putting his hand in his front shirt pocket.

"All right, smart guy," I say, "Put 'em in your pants pockets."

Back out on the sidewalk, a woman with a large dog turns the corner into our path, and Lydia immediately freaks. She hides behind me and clasps my leg. I grab her hand and Alex's and then tell Matt to hold on to the back of the T-shirt I am wearing. We cross the street, literally bound together at my hips and looking vaguely like one of those chemistry models of atoms.

When the dog is past, we have to cross again to get to O'Hara's. We walk around to the kitchen door and even though it's open, I let Alex bang on it a couple of times so that we don't scare anyone who might be inside. Inside, Barb is— skinning a fish? I think that's what she's doing. It's not pleasant to watch, however, so we wave and quickly walk out to the dining room. It's strange to be in the bar when it's empty. It's dark and quiet, but with potential. Like it could erupt at any moment.

We hop up to the bar.

"Hey, Hogan!" I yell. I know he's here because his laptop is set up at the end of the bar. "Where are you?"

He runs down the stairs.

"Hey, Kennedy—why don't you ever call me by my first name?"

"What's your first name again?"

"Ha Ha! You're a riot."

"I don't know. John just doesn't suit you. You look like a Hogan."

"A Hogan is really like an old Indian hut or something. Do I look like a hut?"

"Um . . . do I have to answer that?"

"Hi guys," he says turning his attention to my children. "I'm ignoring your mother. What do you want to drink? A beer?"

"NO!" they shout in unison.

"A whiskey? On the rocks?" He's being cute. He produces three Shirley Temples, extra cherries, as usual.

I grab a newspaper that's on the bar and begin to surf the classifieds for an apartment.

"Find anything yet?"

"No, they're all so expensive."

"Yeah, I know. I was lucky, I found a house out in Searsmont—it's only four hundred a month."

"God, you are lucky. Tell you what, rent it to us and we'll find you an apartment!"

"No deal."

"Pain."

"Yup. You'll find something."

"You keep saying that and yet I have no evidence that it will ever be true."

I circle a couple of possibilities and accept the Diet Coke Hogan has set before me.

"Can I use the phone?"

"God, what else will you want?" But he smiles and puts the cordless phone down in front of me. The kids are on their refills. Mental note: Take kids to bathroom before we leave.

"Excellent," I say, hanging up the phone. "We have a lead on an apartment, but we have to go right now. She's showing it to other people tonight! So I have to get there fast."

"Where is it?"

"Over on Miller Street? Across from a school. The woman said that she has to go over anyway and that she'll meet us there in ten minutes."

"Hey, I did some contracting work over there—it's the Crosby School—it's like a theater school for the handicapped."

"Cool. But we've got to go now. We can walk, can't we?"

"Yeah. Just cross the street and walk up that little hill by the bank. Then make a left. That's Miller Street."

"All right guys, let's go."

"Aw Mom, we don't want to. It's too hot."

"They can stay if they want—we could go for ice cream down the road."

"Yeah, yeah!"

"No, I couldn't let you . . ."

"What's more fun, guys? Apartment shopping or ice cream?"

"John." It felt weird saying his first name. "You don't have to."

"I know. I want to. We'll meet you back here in an hour."

"OK, you guys. Be good. Don't make Hogan mad at you—I've seen him get mad."

"We won't!"

"All right then, bye!" And I head out the door.

On the walk over to the apartment building, I try not to get too excited. I've been through this at least twenty times before and either someone outbids me for the place or they won't accept less for the security deposit. More often than not, they keep looking at my kids, and I can tell they don't want a bunch of little kids in the apartment. The brochure I got from the

Job Center says that's illegal, but it's also difficult to prove that kind of discrimination, especially if I don't have all the cash up front. They can just say that's the reason.

I walk up three flights of outside stairs and walk into the open door. The hall is long and kind of dark in an old house kind of way, but not a creepy Bates Motel way. The wooden hall floor has been painted cornflower blue and is dotted with what appears to be chocolate ice cream. I pass a door to the right, a door to the left, and then a big open staircase with a huge cloudy, unreachable window above it. The door at the end of the hallway is the apartment: 3C.

The door is open and I tentatively walk into the large, old-fashioned kitchen. I half-knock on the door.

"Hello?"

"Yes. I'm here. One second," a voice says. I hear water running, presumably from the bathroom. There is a beautiful built-in china cabinet on my immediate right and a large empty space where a table could go. It's big and empty and clean, and there's carpet on the floor in the tiny living room.

"Sorry," she says, taking rubber dish gloves off her hands. She wipes her hands on her jeans. I shake her hand. "I was cleaning the bathroom. You're Melissa?"

"Michelle. Yes."

"Oh, Michelle, sorry. I'm Mrs. Hopkins, and I own this building and the one next to it. I live downstairs. Now, obviously this is the kitchen. The living room is small, but it will hold a couch and a TV. Here's the bathroom . . ." The bathroom is tiny. Green tile, no windows and only a shower, but I don't care. I look at both bedrooms. One is immense, plenty big for the three kids to share and then there is a smaller room for, well, me.

The same gray, low-pile carpet runs throughout the apartment.

"It's small, but it's nice up here, and in the winter your heating bill will be low, because everyone below you will have theirs on. You said on the phone that you have kids, right?"

"Yes, three." I cringe, hoping she won't send me on my way.

"Are you sure this will be big enough?"

"Oh, yes. They're not very big!" I laugh. "It's a wonderful place, really. I just love it." I am gushing—trying to win her over with my charm, but I can't help it. There is something in the sea air that is wafting into the empty rooms and makes me want to stay.

"What do you do?" she asks. She looks me right in the eye, like one wrong answer could ruin our chances.

I repeat my story of bartending and kids and dogsleds and ramble on for so long about ex-husbands and security deposits on apartments that she finally holds her hand up and says, "Enough. I understand."

"I have enough money saved for the first month's rent and the security deposit," I say. It's $550 a month, a reasonable price for a two-bedroom, and I am confident that once I have a place to lay my head, I can make my budget work.

"I usually try and get the last month's rent too," she says. I look at the ground. Christ. Fuck. Damn. Everyone. Everyone wants it all now.

"I understand," I say. "Thanks for your time . . ."

"Now wait. I didn't say I expected it every time. Where do you work?"

"Just over there," I say pointing out the window at O'Hara's—a little spring back in my step. "At O'Hara's."

"For Lyle?"

"Yes."

"So if I call him, he'll say something nice about you?"

"I hope so."

"All right. If you'll sign a year lease, we'll go with what you've got. That's eleven hundred dollars."

"I brought it with me."

"Rent is due by the fifth of every month—after that I charge a late fee. There's no laundry here—you'll have to go to the Laundromat—do you know where that is?"

"Yes, ma'am."

"Water is included, but you have to pay for your heat and electricity—they're the same bill. I'll call them and put it all in your name."

"That would be wonderful, thank you."

"When will you move in?"

"Um . . . how about now?"

"Whatever. Here's your key. I'll be downstairs if you need anything."

"Wow. Thanks. That was quick."

"I hate renting apartments, so when I find someone nice, I like to get it done. Now, I have to go cancel some appointments. Bring your kids down to meet me later."

"Yes, ma'am."

"Stop calling me that."

And that's it. After three months of living in the car, from the middle of May to now, the middle of August, we have a place to live. We're not homeless anymore. We're busted broke, but we have a place to sleep and, well, live. All it took was one nice person willing to just take a chance. Just one and our life is completely different. I am ecstatic. I actually skip all of the way back to the bar.

"We have an apartment!" I yell to the kids—completely unaware that bar is now full of people. They're at a table eating—again.

"Great!" Hogan says, but motions hands so that I'll shut up. "That wasn't too hard."

"Yeah, no sweat," I say. "God, do kids ever stop eating?"

"I don't think so—wait until the boys are teenagers."

"Can we go now?" Matt asks.

"Yes, we can," I say. "Hogan, thank you so much—for watching the guys. I appreciate it. I'll see you tomorrow."

"Wait a sec," he says. "You got a phone call while you were out. A 'Tom' said he'd be here tomorrow afternoon around one and to meet him here."

"At the bar?"

"I guess."

"Did he leave a phone number?"

"No."

"Can I have the phone?" I call our old number in Belton. It's disconnected. Wonderful. I slam the phone down.

"Who's Tom?"

"My soon-to-be-ex-husband."

"Oh." He's just staring at me.

"Well, on that happy note—we have an apartment to go and populate."

"Need any help?"

"Nah, I don't have that much to move—it's all in the car! Thanks again!" I gather up the kids and we walk back to the car. Time to go be normal. I decide that I won't think about Tom until tomorrow morning. What great timing. As soon as I get a place, he calls. It's almost as if he's psychic. Where was he a month ago? And how did he get my number? Never mind, I know the answer to that. He probably called my parents.

I follow the kids up the stairs and into the building. I am carrying our TV set and am grateful for the constant work-out I've gotten at O'Hara's, carrying full trays and bus tubs up and down the stairs. I plug in the set. The reception is lousy, but there is Barney, bright and purple, if not a bit fuzzy, sing-ing out to us. The children are mesmerized and I am able to run out to the car and get the rest of our things.

It doesn't take long for me to set everything up. I put the few dishes in the china cabinet. They look lonely, my few dishes, in a cabinet prepared for so much more. A fry pan, a soup pot. Some silverware—mismatched utensils I have gar-nered from yard sales. I set the kids' comforters out and make them little beds. I make myself a bed on the floor—sleeping bag underneath and comforter on top. I organize our clothes in the closets, giving each of us a Rubbermaid tub as a dresser. I set our toothbrushes out in the bathroom.

It looks almost homey. I lie down in the living room next to the kids and just soak up the ambience of our new home.

After a celebratory hour of lying on the floor and watching PBS, I realize we have very little food aside from ramen noo-dles and a bag of apples. I have about a hundred dollars left and am assured of making at least that much on my Sunday afternoon at work tomorrow, I feel free to go to the store— although I am limiting myself to fifty dollars. The IGA is within walking distance of the apartment, and lacking a desire to get in my car again, we walk.

I am giddy with delight as I pick up concentrated orange juice, a bag of oranges, and pears, a box of Toasty O's, the generic Cheerio. I forgot what it was like to shop for more than one day at a time. I know that fifty dollars doesn't sound like a lot to shop with, but I am the queen of frugal shopping. Big bags of egg noodles, frozen veggies—we are pasta connoisseurs. I buy lots of different shapes to jazz things up. Meat is expensive so I buy a big package of chicken leg quarters to roast. Granola bars are cheap, and they can serve as both snack and dessert. We buy flour and sugar to make our own cookies. Someday, I think, someday I will buy all kinds of things—but when I think about it further, if you have the storage space, buying cheap is also a pretty healthy way to eat. A lot of the convenience food is overprocessed and expensive, so even if I can afford it, I probably won't buy it. But it's fun to fantasize. As a treat, I buy the kids a box of Oreos—double stuffed, of course—and a bag of Pepperidge Farm Orange Milanos for me. They are the ultimate decadence to me and I feel like this is the time to splurge.

I happily hand over my forty-five dollars, and we carry our booty back to the apartment. Lydia is determined to make it the whole three blocks carrying a gallon of milk. She struggles a little and people on the street look at me like I'm a slave driver, prompting me to say things like, "Are you sure *you* want to carry that, Sweetie?" and "I'll carry it for you if you want," entirely too loud, so people will know that she wants to do it.

On our way up the stairs, Mrs. Hopkins comes out of her apartment.

"Come on down when you're done. I made some cookies for your little ones," she says. Immediately my don't-talk-to-strangers instinct kicks in—a remnant of walking home from school in the 'burbs, I'm sure. We kids were always told never to go into anyone's house when we were selling Girl Scout cookies, never to take anything from strangers, and that if anything bad happened to rush to a house with a helping hand.

This was a little hand-shaped sign in the window signifying a good neighbor who would take in a scared child—no matter that the hand signs were practically given out on the street and that any pervert could put one in their window.

But I assured myself that Mrs. Hopkins had no desire to harm us. How would she get her rent otherwise? And so we put our groceries away and then head to the downstairs apartment.

Lydia confidently knocks on the large, red front door. The knocker, too tall for Lydia to reach, is a pineapple. My father once told me that pineapples are supposed to bring good luck when you place them on the front door. I'm not very superstitious, but far be it from me to look the gift of luck in the face, so I make another mental note to get a pineapple for my door.

Mrs. Hopkins opens the door and we walk into a large foyer, where she instructs us all to take off our shoes. At first, I am a little put off by the assumption that we must not have wiped our feet at the door, but the real reason soon becomes clear. Mrs. Hopkins, herself in stocking feet, has beautiful hardwood floors covered in ancient oriental rugs. The rugs barely look worn—no doubt from a lifetime under the stocking feet of Mrs. Hopkins.

"Don't touch anything," I whisper harshly in Matthew's and then Lydia's ear. Then I set Alex on the floor, remove his Elmo Velcro sneakers, and swoop him up onto my hip, so that I can control his every move.

"Now, come into the kitchen," we hear from down the dark hall. As we shuffle down the hall, past sideboards with framed pictures of what appear to be Mrs. Hopkins's relatives and children, I realize that the whole first floor belongs to her. The hall follows the same pattern as our hallway two floors above, but instead of being divided into apartments it is divided into massive rooms. In the corner of one table, elevated on several antique books—the kind one keeps for show rather than for reading, like an 1830s copy of *Sugaring with Oxen*—is a picture of a little girl with pitch-black hair and eyes almost as dark. She looks like one of the pictures they show on the TV commercials for the Christian Children's Fund. The kitchen is at the end of the hall, illuminated by french doors that open out onto a veranda that overlooks the small, fenced-in backyard— well landscaped of course. I fear that we have walked into a Martha Stewart book, but gratefully accept the glass of lemonade that is placed in my hand.

"Have a seat," Mrs. Hopkins says. We sit. The kids are a little fearful of all of this grandeur and formality and sit with their hands folded in their laps—even Alex—awaiting whatever will happen next. Pieces of chicken potpie are placed on plates before them, and they start to dig in when Mrs. Hopkins scolds them for having poor manners.

"Don't you know that it's impolite to eat before everyone is served?" she asks. Matthew carefully places his fork down next to his plate, and Lydia looks like she's going to cry.

"I'm sorry," I say to Mrs. Hopkins, more than a little agitated that she would dare to hurt my babies' feelings.

"I think they were just excited by the wonderful meal you made—they know better, right guys?" I certainly don't want things here to get off to a bad start before we've even been here a day. The kids smile and nod their heads up and down— they know too well how to kiss up. It works on me all the time. But I smile back proudly and ruffle Matthew on the head. Cutting up Alex's portion, I notice that Mrs. Hopkins is suddenly very quiet.

"Are you OK?" I ask her. "We haven't done something wrong, have we?"

"No, no." she says shaking her head slowly. "I'm sorry. I'm just not used to having kids in the house."

"It's fine," I say, trying to be reassuring. "I forget how crazy we must all seem. I'm used to all the noise, but don't think there aren't times when I wish I could go hide somewhere."

Mrs. Hopkins titters. I never really knew what it meant to titter until I heard her laugh. It's funny the way her little mouth curls together as the little hoo, hoos come out. Her face is quite round, so she reminds me of the pictures of carolers on Christmas cards, with their mouths formed in a perfect O shape. Her hair is long and gray with a few streaks of white, and she has pulled what appears to be quite a mass of it into a loose bun on the top of her head.

After dinner, Matthew and Lydia clear the table without me asking them to. I am stunned, but I think they want all of this normalcy to last as long as possible. Mrs. Hopkins tells them to take Alex into the backyard to play while we have grown-up talk. They happily oblige and are soon running through the huge backyard, throwing not yet ripe apples that have fallen off the trees to each other and playing hide and seek. Pouring me a cup of tea, Mrs. Hopkins sits down next to me at the table, and for a few moments, we are silent, watching the children through the door. I decide to make the first attempt at grown-up conversation.

"Have you lived here all of your life?" I ask.

"Oh, heavens no," she replies. "But it seems like it's been forever. I grew up in New York City. I still go back there sometimes. I like to go before the holidays—it gets me in the Christmas spirit."

We talked for an hour or two. Well, she talked, but I loved listening. Mrs. Hopkins had a life filled with adventure—something I wouldn't have imagined just by walking into her apartment. She was a Native American woman in the Air Force at a time when not many women chose the military as a way of life. She traveled all over Europe during her time in the service with her husband and their growing family. After Europe, the family spent time in Texas where she worked for the social service division and aided migrant farmworkers and their families. It was an amazing story and I wanted to sit and listen to her talk about it for hours.

"Come with me and I'll show you some other great pictures," she says, leading me into a sitting room off the dining room. I take a peek at the kids and determine that they will be fine for a minute. They are now sitting under a large tree. It looks like they are planning some sort of game. Lydia is obviously in charge, giving Matthew and Alex instructions.

"Now be careful of the loom, it's in a precarious state right now as I am threading it so I can begin on my next piece," she says. Filling the room, almost from floor to ceiling and just as wide, was a huge floor loom. Underneath it was a large Navaho-style rug. I hadn't really noticed before, but it appeared that all of the floors were covered with some sort of rag rug—obviously handmade. On the wall was one large piece that resembled an impressionist painting. The colors were all reds, golds, and rusts; and the yarn was very shiny and soft looking. I leaned over to feel it.

"Hey! Don't touch!" Mrs. Hopkins yells from behind me. I spin around with my hands clasped behind my back like a naughty girl caught red-handed.

"I'm sorry, I just wanted to see if it felt as soft as it looks," I stammer.

"I can assure you that it does," she says. "Now, if you are done feeling everything, I can show you the pictures we came in for."

"Yes, ma'am," I say. Mrs. Hopkins is standing next to a row of bookshelves that have been built specifically for this wall. They reach all of the way to the ceiling and the four bottom shelves are enclosed cabinets. The ladder is painted maroon to match the shelves and is hitched to a rail at the top so that you could lift the bottom and roll the ladder to whatever part of the shelf you need to reach. I am a little glad that the kids are outside and have not yet seen this piece of play equipment. But I also put this type of shelf on my mental list for the dream house I am secretly building in my head.

Pulling a small box out of one of the cabinets, Mrs. Hopkins sets it down on the cedar trunk in the center of the room and points to a chair for me to sit in. It's a lovely old chair, just the kind I always wanted to have if I owned a bookstore. It's overstuffed with maroon velvet upholstery. The back is high and thronelike and the arms are slender but with just enough of the velvety padding to make one's arm comfortable. I feel like a queen sitting in it, but Mrs. Hopkins soon put me in my place.

"Now, open it up," she commands. "The first envelope is pictures of my husband and me on the Cape." And on it went, picture after picture, until I heard pounding at the back door.

"I, um, think the kids are probably done playing outside," I say, gently putting the pictures back in their box.

"Well, in my day, a child was told when they were done playing, not the other way around," she says.

"I try to be a little lenient," I say. "Especially with everything they have been through; besides, I can already tell that they love it here."

This pleases her, and so she lets the kids in while I clear up the pictures. One family picture falls on the floor and as I bend down to pick it up, I notice that the same little girl—the dark-haired one—that I saw in the hall was in this picture. Obviously, she isn't a charity case, but a part of the family. All over the house there are pictures of Mrs. Hopkins's other children—all grown—and with her grandchildren, but there didn't seem to be any more pictures of this little girl.

The kids are brushing the grass off their feet as I walk into the kitchen. The quiet apartment is now filled with chatter, and I can tell that Mrs. Hopkins is trying to look annoyed, but isn't.

"Did you know you have a squirrel family living in the oak tree back there?" Matthew asks. "We watched them find acorns and other stuff and take it up there. When we lay down on the grass, we could watch them jump from tree to tree to tree without even touching the ground. It's like they have their own highway up there."

"Indeed," Mrs. Hopkins says smiling a little. "A squirrel highway—next you'll tell me that the birds have an airport."

"Maybe," Lydia says thoughtfully. "Do you think? Mama—I'm gonna draw a picture of a bird highway."

"All right," I reply. "As soon as we get . . ." and I pause for a second, "home." I had almost forgotten that we had one.

"Now, before you go, I have something to ask you two, Matthew and Lydia," Mrs. Hopkins says. "Occasionally I have need of a couple extra pairs of hands to do things like help me rake the yard, bake pies for the bake sale at the church, clean the basement, that kind of thing. Would either of you two be interested in such work if I paid, say fifty cents cents an hour?"

"Each?" Matt and Lydia reply in unison.

"Yes, if you do a good job," Mrs. Hopkins says. "I'll tell you what—tomorrow's a Sunday, after church . . ."

"But we don't go to church," Matthew says.

"Well, I do—and you should think about it," she says. I try to keep from rolling my eyes, but keep my comments to myself. "But when I get back, then you two come over here and we'll see what kind of leaf rakers you are."

"Cool," Matthew says. "But do you have an extra rake? I don't have one."

"Indeed I do, don't you worry, and tools are provided on this job."

"And so with that, you three, we should be going," I say. "It is getting very close to bedtime."

"We had a wonderful time," I say to Mrs. Hopkins as she sees us out her red door. "You have been more than kind, and I think the kids feel like they have found a new friend."

"No trouble at all," she says. "Oh, and welcome home."

Thirteen

I wake up with an awful twisting and turning in my stomach at about 4:00 A.M. I'm sweating and nervous and one thought is penetrating my brain: He's coming. Oh, Christ, why does he have to come today? I almost feel like I would be better off if I never saw him again. I don't want to face him. I don't want anything that even vaguely reminds me of him.

I hate my anxiety attacks. I've always had them, ever since I was in high school. They used to scare me. I would wake up at three or four in the morning and remember a paper I hadn't finished or a test I would undoubtedly fail. I've gotten better about it as I've gotten older. Now, I can focus my brain and tell myself that there is nothing I can do about whatever problem I'm obsessing over. Usually it's money. Back in Maryland, it was always money. What would I tell the electric company? Or the phone company? What lie could I make up that would keep our service going and buy us a little extra time? Tom never worried about such things. He always slept well.

I fall asleep again and wake up at 8:00 A.M. to a huge wet Alex kiss. Matt and Lydia are already making their cereal. They are so excited to be able to do it themselves. It's little things like this that make having a home seem more real. Matthew brings the milk to me in bed so that I can pull the plastic ring off the top. He pours the milk for the three of them. He spills some, but I don't care. I throw him the roll of paper towels, left behind after the Mrs. Hopkins cleaning frenzy, and he wipes it up. I realize we don't have a garbage can yet, so I set up one of the grocery bags in the corner.

"Hey, guess what, guys?" I say in my most chipper of un-coffee-induced voices. "Your dad is supposed to meet us at Mommy's work today. Isn't that cool?"

Lydia dances. Alex claps and Matt just looks down at his cereal.

"What's the matter, buddy?"

"I don't want him to come."

"Why not? Haven't you missed him?"

"Not really."

"Wanna talk about it?"

"I just don't want him to come."

"OK. Well, he's going to come, but you don't have to hang out with him or anything, OK?"

"OK."

"Well, let's not think about that now anyway. I thought we'd hit a couple of yard sales and see if we could find us some furniture."

Most of the stuff at the yard sales is picked over by now although it's only 9:00 A.M., but we find a nice recliner that still kind of reclines for five dollars and a record player. One of the other things I had hidden in my stash of stuff was five of my old record albums—James Taylor's *Sweet Baby James*, Jimmy Buffet's *Margaritaville*, and the Beatles' *Sgt. Pepper*, *Rubber Soul*, and *Abbey Road*. Five albums guaranteed to get me through almost anything. The kids and I like to clean to Jimmy Buffet, and my father turned me on to James Taylor—his obsession with the song "Sweet Baby James," being somewhat of a legend in my family.

For as long as I can remember my father played records on either Friday or Saturday of every week. He'd dig out all kinds of stuff: The Beatles; Rolling Stones; Bob Dylan—the standards. Then he'd get out the Moody Blues, the Kingston Trio, and Billy Joel for my mother. Don McLean was always in there somewhere. As was Jimmy Buffet. And then there was James Taylor. After "Fire and Rain" and "Carolina on My Mind," there was the requisite three—maybe four playings of "Sweet Baby James." And so we would sit, my mother, my sisters, and I and whoever had been fortunate enough to be along for the ride. Every weekend. We drank, we smoked—OK, they smoked—we ate, and we argued ourselves blue. And it was usually fun. Sometimes I got so angry over whatever we were arguing about that I would run out of the house. But I always went back. And everything was fine again. My soon-to-be-ex-husband could never understand that we argued for fun. That we were solving the world's problems right there at my mother's kitchen table among the pasta and the wine and cheap beer and the Camel Lights. And the next weekend, we'd all switch sides.

There was something about being at O'Hara's that reminded me of those times. Maybe that's why I like it there.

I sit in the new recliner, which I have coaxed the boy who mows the lawn around the apartment into helping me lug up the stairs, and read the Sunday papers. It's hot. Sweaty, disgusting, sit-still-and-pant-like-a-dog hot. Matt and Lyd are in the kitchen trying to get Alex to walk across it. He has not yet managed more than twenty consecutive steps, something of a late bloomer in walking.

The local Sunday paper takes about thirty seconds to get through. It is the thickness of just one section of the *New York Times*, but I try and glean as much out of it as possible.

Reading the Sunday paper is an experience for me. It's not just information, but a fantasy where I envision whole new lives for myself. Flipping through the want ads I can see the choices: marine biologist, teacher, bartender, computer specialist, waitress, engineer—and while it does occur to me that I am only qualified for a couple of these positions, the possibilities seem endless.

The possibilities seemed very real on this day when I read: "Wanted: friendly people to help large credit card company. Excellent pay and benefits."

Something in me clicks. I know I have to try for a job there. It's a well-known credit card company in the financial world, but they are still just making their initial strides in this small community. For a town that repeatedly rejects Wal-Mart, it seems strange that this large company is able to make its foothold so strong, but a couple of well-placed donations and a new gymnasium for the school have certainly smoothed the way.

Of course, at the bar, Barb, Steve, Lyle, Jay, Hogan, and I

constantly make fun of the new executives who come in, bitching about the lack of things to do and the mud on their new leather shoes. But there is a part of me that envies them. I envy their money and their job security. I even envy their professionalism. This is what grown-ups are supposed to do—what they are supposed to be. I should have to wear a suit every day, and I should be able to sit in a chair and work on a computer. I should not deal with drunks and wring the smell of beer out of my socks every night. A job like that would enable me to support my children in the manner they deserve—a stable one. I will work for the credit card company.

Invigorated with a new enthusiasm, and with a desire to keep my mind off Tom's impending visit, the kids and I take off down the street to search the thrift store for something appropriate to wear to the company's job fair the next week. I am always shocked at the great things I find in thrift stores. I used to refuse to shop in them, back in the days when the sound of the muffler on my Dad's Wagoneer embarrassed me to no end—I thought they smelled, but I don't care now. I can't remember the last time I bought clothes at retail.

Inside Twice Is Nice, I sift through the business wear section. It's a hodgepodge of blazers and those fashionable women's blouses they call shells, usually satin and frilly, to go underneath the selected blazer. A double-breasted black blazer peeks out at me from behind a horrible green dress. Combined with black pants and a button-down white shirt I found for a quarter, I am able to keep my ensemble to under $5. Not exactly the demographic the credit card company would be selling to, but I hope I look the part at least.

My $20 budget allows me to spend my last $15 on shoes. I decide to go to a regular shoe store, because there is something about wearing used shoes that just bugs me. With used clothes, the smell of the previous owner is easily washed away, but you can never clean away the former imprint of someone else's foot. I'd rather have cheap new shoes than well-made used ones. As I pick through the shoes on clearance, I wonder if that is some kind of strange reverse snobbery.

Completely outfitted for the job fair, I look at my watch. One o'clock.

Tom is sitting at the bar when we walk in. Jay is serving him a beer. The kids run up to him and hug him, even Matt. He is tan and healthy looking. His hair is much longer than the crew cut I remember. His body is the same thin, muscular one I slept next to for so long. Almost eight years.

I ask Jay to put my bags behind the bar.

"Hey," is all I can think of.

"How are you?" he asks.

"We're great," I say, a little too enthusiastically. I sound like Tony the Tiger.

"So, um . . . I have some great news," he says.

"Really? Why don't we take a walk and you can tell me all about it?"

We gather up the kids and they lead us down toward the beach. They are skipping ahead and running around signposts. We don't talk during the walk. But it feels strangely comfortable. Distant, but comfortable.

We pick a large piece of driftwood to sit on and the kids set about playing in the surf—their main duty to bring us every piece of sea glass or shell they find. We examine each one with great detail.

"So, what's your news?" I ask, fearing the answer.

"I found a great piece of land right nearby. I've already set up a tent and the few dogs I have left. I'm going to start building a house by hand, and we can garden and . . ."

"Whoa—hold on. Who we?"

"Us we. Me and you and the kids."

"I can't do that again. We just got an apartment—with running water and electricity—and I like it."

"Well, you can live there while I build the house."

"I don't know, Tom. I don't think I want to live that way again."

"Why not?"

"It's just . . . am I a wuss if I say it's just too hard? I like having my water come out of a faucet. I like flipping a switch and having a light turn on. Christ, I even like TV. And I think the kids deserve a normal life, at least for now, while they're this young. I don't think I can go back to that. I'm trying for a new job this week and . . ."

"Well you can still work and all that, but the kids can help me on the land."

"I don't think so. It's just too dangerous, isn't it?"

"No, I don't know. I guess. So then what?"

"I think I want a divorce." I have never said the words out loud before. It feels strange to hear them come out now. I haven't thought about an actual divorce until now. I've been too busy and the logistics of it haven't crossed my mind.

"OK," he says. Just like that. "OK."

I wish he would put up a bit of a fight. But if there is one thing I have learned about Tom over the years, it's that he's not a fighter. If I wanted to stay, great. If not, I could go. There wasn't going to be any grand proclamation of love. No begging me to live with him forever. And I wanted him to. I wanted him to say, "I can't live without you guys, I will do whatever it takes to make you happy. I'll get a good job. I'll live in a normal house."

But he couldn't, or wouldn't, say those things. It's not the life he wants. He wants to live off the land and garden and be self-sufficient. And while I admire his conviction, I hate that I'm not worth it. After eight years and three kids and so many nights lying in the snow looking at the stars, we have come to this. An impasse. The word *divorce* is still hanging between us and yet somehow, it feels like the best idea I've ever had.

"Come on," I say, trying not to show how hurt I am. "I'll show you our new apartment."

We walk up the hill to Miller Street and I proudly show Tom our new home. He nods and acts pleased for the children. He's obviously not. He thinks it's all some sort of succumbing to the horrors of modern life. Whatever. I'm pleased. And to show just how pleased I am, I order pizza.

"See," I say, teasing him, "it comes right to the door."

We eat on the kitchen floor and I feel remarkably like a family again. The kids go off to play in their room, and I start to think about how this whole divorce thing will work. He agrees to pay me some child support as soon as he finds a job— a job, I can hardly believe he's considering it—and then we start talking about visitation rights. I never thought I would have to think about things like this. But at the same time, we are trying to be very cool about it. No fights. Kids will stay with me. All of that.

He offers to babysit at night while I'm at work. Just like that he's back in our lives. It almost seems like he waited until I got the apartment. Like somehow he knew.

We agree to try it for a couple of days and see how it works out. Then it appears to be time for him to leave. And we stand there, looking at each other. Unsure of how to say good-bye. It all seems so surreal. Ending a marriage this way. He leans down and kisses me. It's the most passion I've felt from this man in years. I lead him to the bedroom, and we sleep together.

When I wake up in the morning, I know it's over. He leaves and agrees to come back before my shift later that day. He hugs the kids good-bye and even Matthew is happy that he's coming back. I feel almost indifferent about it.

The kids and I spend the day playing and loafing, and we talk a little about Tom. I continually wince at myself for sleeping with him. I can't believe I'm so weak, but at the same time I suddenly feel free of him.

I teach Matt how to use the phone to call me at work and dial 911.

"If it's really bad, call 911," I repeat over and over. I also make him recite our address in case he needs to give it out. I really feel like I'm going out on a limb letting Tom watch the kids, especially after everything that has happened, but somehow I feel enlightened by doing so. Giving him a chance to make amends, at least that's what I think he's doing. Somehow I feel like I am being the bigger person here, as if I am blameless for the whole situation. I know better than this, but I can't admit to it—not yet.

Tom shows up late but I don't make a big deal out of it. I kiss my babies and for the first time since Lydia's accident, I leave them with Tom. I am nervous as hell but try not to show it.

I walk into the coolness of the bar and sit on a stool directly facing Hogan.

"I am the dumbest person in the universe," I say.

"Yeah . . . and . . ."

"I slept with my soon-to-be-ex-husband last night."

"Why?"

"I don't know—good-bye maybe?"

"Desperate maybe."

"Yeah."

"Don't worry about it—I for one am the king of poor judgment."

"I am the queen of bad judgment."

"Nah, I bet I still beat you."

"What could you have possibly done that's worse than living in a car and sleeping with your ex?"

He walks out from behind the bar and sits by the front door on the bottom two steps. He wipes his sweaty forehead with the dishtowel he keeps on his shoulder. It reminds me of the spit-up rags I kept on my shoulder when the kids needed to burp.

It's deathly slow tonight. Mondays always are. George is at the bar. Barb is in the kitchen. And Hogan and I are sitting on the stairs, trying to catch a bay breeze through the front door.

We talk. The first real conversation we have ever had. He tells me about being married once himself, about living in Ireland, about his girlfriend. Customers drizzle in and out. We serve them and keep talking. On the stairs. At the bar. He tells me about old girlfriends. Old wounds. And I am genuinely interested and amazed by this man and all that he's done. He's taught Shakespeare classes. He's ridden his bike across Ireland.

Between Mrs. Hopkins and Hogan and their amazing stories, I feel miniscule. I have accomplished nothing. I've done nothing even remotely important or interesting.

"I'm off to the credit card company tomorrow," I say while I clean up for closing. "Any inspirational words?"

"Yeah. Why do you want to work there?" Hogan asks.

"I don't know. Money's good and steady—not like here. They have air-conditioning, health insurance, and day care assistance. Matt starts school in the fall and I'd like to have something steady going."

"Makes sense, I guess. We'd miss you around here though."

"Well, first, I haven't even gotten the job yet; and second, I only live around the corner—I'll be able to bug you all the time."

"True enough. Come in when you're done, let us know how you did."

"All right. I'll see you tomorrow."

As I walk home, those words of his from my birthday are still ringing in my ears: "In three years, you are the only person who has ever made me consider leaving my girlfriend."

I wonder if it's still true.

Tom appears to have kept everyone in good shape while I was at work, even if the kitchen looks as though a bomb hit it. I wake him from the chair and tell him he can go. The TV's on and he appears to have taken a shower. Nice to have lofty simplicity morals when your ex-wife has running water. I'll take care of the dishes in the morning. I smile. Guess I can't expect too much to have changed. But I feel violated somehow, though. I know he has a right to see his children, and I want to give him that, but at the same time I feel like this is our private sanctuary, and I don't want him invading that space. Maybe I'll talk to Diane about it after the interview.

In the morning, I dress up in my thrift-store best.

"Ooh," Lydia says. "You look pretty. Where are you going?"

"Are you wearing makeup, Mom?" Matthew asks. "You never wear makeup."

"I do sometimes," I say. "I am going to see about a new job

in a big office, and I thought it would be nice if I tried to look a little prettier than I usually do."

"You'll be the prettiest lady there," Lydia says. Alex and Matthew just look at me funny. And I feel awful when I immediately push Alex aside as he tries to hug me with his toast- and jelly-covered arms. Alex sits down on the floor and cries.

"Oh, I'm sorry," I say, almost crying myself. "I'm just trying to keep my pants clean. Here, let's wipe you off, and then I'll read you a story before we go to Diane's."

Putting my freshly wiped child on my lap in my little abode, I think about the millions of mothers who are also getting their children ready for day care this morning. Do they get as anal as I do about being touched with jellied hands in their work clothes? How many of them stay home and see their husbands off at the door with a lunch and a kiss? How many of them are in an apartment with their three children alone, washing clothes in the sink and hanging them on the shower curtain rod so they can save $5 at the Laundromat? Not so many, I bet. But I bet there are more than I think there are.

I drop the kids off at Diane's and they yell "Good luck!" to me from the porch, although I'm not sure they know what they are wishing me luck for.

I try desperately not to look as embarrassed as I feel while I drive around the bank's parking lot looking for a space. My car makes a horribly loud putt-putt sound, ranging in speed proportionally to the pressure my foot puts on the clutch. I pull the rusting, yet somehow still surviving Subaru into place next to the largest SUV I have ever seen. I try to remember the placement of both cars in this monstrously big lot, because I am sure that from far away, I will only be able to view the SUV if it is still there when I get back.

Walking across the parking lot, I try and avoid the puddles from the previous night's rain with some amount of grace and style in my new one-inch heels, but I eventually give up on the grace and style and settle for getting my teetering self in the doors without getting wet. I can't remember the last time I wore heels; I have lived in my sneakers for so long. I follow a leggy blonde in a short skirt into the building, admiring her adept walking skills and trying desperately to imitate them.

The building is enormous. I enter the atrium and am immediately struck by the sound of a piano. It is not loud, but it provides the perfect background to what I now believe to be the perfect company to employ me. I am not alone. There are hundreds of other reasonably well-dressed locals gazing up and down at the higher than cathedral ceilings, illuminated by the skylights and windows that run from ceiling to floor. While craning my neck at the glass elevator, I locate the piano player who is at what I later learn is the mezzanine level. I am in awe that a place of such grandeur could exist in such a do-nothing town.

A voice from above tells all of us hopefuls to fill in the forms located at a table in the back of the room and then to please sit and wait to be called. While we wait, huge television screens are lowered in front of each set of sofas and chairs, arranged living-room style, and we watch a video on the greatness of working for the bank. I am immediately turned off by the herd mentality in the video, set on permanent loop. I hate this sort of rah-rah thinking, but have decided to go against my gut and persevere in this opportunity because it is what grown-ups do.

"Work is just work," my father says in my head again. "If it were fun, they'd call it fun. But it's not, it's work." I fought with my father intensely on this point for many years. But it's his mantra, and I can't get it out of my head.

"That's not true!" I would shout. "You can make money and do what you love . . . I could write or be a musician!"

"How many ads for Rock Star do you see in the paper, Michelle? Sooner or later, you will have to get a regular job and be like the rest of us."

And here I am, ten years later. Twenty-five years old. Three kids. No money. Just barely in a home of our own. No career. No husband. I have to get this job. This has to be my chance at a real life.

My name is called with about fifteen others, and we are shunted through the brilliantly lit atrium down a dark hallway, incandescently lit, to a small conference room with a large round table. The perky leader of our little group can't be more than twenty-two. She's a lifer—I can just tell. They got her early. They got her right out of college and instilled in her the virtues of the bank. She probably plays on the softball team, puts the maximum contribution in her 401K, and donates her spare time to feed homeless people in the bank shelter— passing out credit card applications on her walk there.

I stand up and smile, falling into line with the other new recruits. I fight the cynical comments churning through my head, reminding myself that I want this job. Our perky leader informs us that we have been selected to apply for the customer retention section, based on our applications. I wonder what section of my application makes me best suited for customer retention—the waiting tables part or the housewife part?

The tour was enlightening. A lot of cubicles. Every hall we went down turned off into another large room filled with cubicles.

"I wonder," I whisper to the woman in front of me, "will there be cheese at the end of this tour?" Does no one see the humor in that joke? Sheesh. She isn't amused, but the guy behind me is. We make crude jokes about the peril of cubicles and the Valley Girl leading us around for the rest of the tour. The unamused woman keeps turning around and glaring at us. I poke my buddy with my elbow and ask him if he thinks it would always be like this, like school. We introduce ourselves and amuse each other with silly smirks throughout the rest of the tour.

"All right, folks," our tour guide says. "We are now entering the cafeteria. Please take what you'd like for lunch, on us today, and come sit at the table marked CUSTOMER RETENTION." She made those little curly-q quote signs with her fingers when she said "Customer Retention."

"Come on, Tim. Let's go get some lunch."

Finally, after more inane bank conversation, we have actual job interviews. This is not, Tim tells me at lunch, a time to show too much individuality.

"Just enough to show them you can think, but not too much that you can't be guided by their ultimate wisdom. My brother Phil works in customer service and he's trying to give me as many tips as possible."

"So, if you don't mind me asking, why do you want to work here?"

"Well, my family owns a farm outside of Augusta. Things are really good during maple sugar season, but then it drops off. My mom is in a bad way since she had a stroke so since I can't put her on my insurance, I'm trying to make enough for her medical bills. Phil, he's making enough to feed us all and pay the mortgage my father took out against the farm before he died.

"He really wanted to make the farm into a tourist attraction, y'know? Petting zoo, maple syrup tours, hay rides—the whole thing. He even wanted llamas. He died of a heart attack while tapping a tree last spring. And then my mom had her stroke right after. So between the funeral and, well, you get the picture."

"Jesus," I say. "I don't even know what to say, that must be so hard. But you look like you're up to the task. I'm glad to know at least that you didn't say Customer Retention when your fourth grade teacher asked you what you wanted to be when you grew up!"

He laughs. I never know what to say to people when they tell me their stories. I love to hear them. It's just that, when they're done, I don't want to sound trite in my response. So, I usually try and end the conversation on a laugh. I wonder sometimes if I'm lacking empathy when I do this. I sometimes feel their pain so acutely that I know I wouldn't want anyone crying for me.

I am interrupted from my conversation with Tim by a prim lady wearing a suit that puts my thrift-store wear to shame. She calls my name and leads me through still more cubicles—although these are a lovely shade of mauve, as opposed to the steel gray I have seen everywhere else—into a square office in the back corner of this particular floor. There are windows, floor to ceiling, on every wall of the office except the back wall, which is lined with faux wood shelving. Two walls of windows look out onto the cubicles and the other looks out over the parking lot. It's the first time since I have entered the enormous building that I have some idea of where I am. Inside is a short man, just beginning to bald, who looks quite possibly the same age as I am. It hadn't occurred to me until this moment that there were people in the world my age who had made something of themselves already. There were doctors, lawyers, and this guy, who have all finished school and become professional people—real people, in the real world.

"You can go right in," the lady says.

"Thanks," I reply. The nameplate on the door says FREDERICK MORELAND in bold black letters. He rises from behind his desk when he hears my hand on the doorknob.

"Ms. Kennedy," he says. "Please sit down and tell me all the reasons why you want to work for us."

Oh God. But I am an expert bullshit artist and without too much trouble and a continuous smile, I leave that day—almost five hours after arriving—with my first professional job. I start in a week and I'll make $12 an hour—the most I have ever made in my life, except on a really good night at the bar.

I call Diane from the payphone in the vestibule, but there's a message for me instead. Diane has taken the kids to the beach because it's so hot. They are going to have dinner at the bayside restaurant. They won't be back until 7:00 P.M. or so.

All this good news and no one to share it with. I go back to the bar. I should feel good about having the afternoon completely free, but I don't. Maybe I could drink a frozen mudslide very slowly.

Hogan's working the bar as usual. He's preparing for the evening. There will be music, so even though it's a Tuesday, it might prove to be a busy one. I hop behind the bar and help him wash the dishes.

"I got the job, Hogan," I say.

"I can see down your shirt Kennedy," he replies.

"Pervert." But I don't move out of view quickly. For some reason the thought of him getting a thrill looking down my shirt gives me a thrill.

I will miss working here. I like working for Hogan and

Lyle. They are relatively easy to please. As long as everything is clean, they don't care if I sit down when there aren't customers around—or if it's just George. I had worked in plenty of places in my life where they did care about your every working move. In the nightclub in Belton, Maine, even if the place was empty and prepared for a crowd, I was still expected to always be cutting fruit or sweeping something or wiping something down. The place had apparently adopted the "idle hands are the devil's work" policy. However, when you're only making two dollars an hour, it seems like in the slow times one should be able to relax a bit more before the onslaught of crying customers. I've never understood how restaurants can get away with only paying two dollars an hour. It's been explained to me a thousand times: "You can make ten to fifteen dollars an hour when it's really busy," they say. But if you average it all out, it's still barely a living wage. And it's some of the hardest work in the world.

I have drifted back to the other side of the bar, and Hogan leans down in front of me. Before he can say anything, I ask, "Do you think I'm crazy to let Tom watch the kids while I'm working?"

"Yes," he says.

"What?"

"Yes, I think you're crazy to let Tom babysit."

"Why? He's their father."

"Only when it's convenient for him."

I am stunned by this.

"What do you mean?" I ask.

"I mean, after everything you have told me and everything you've complained about, it seems like it's awful convenient for him to be a father now that you've got an apartment and everything."

"Yeah, but . . ."

"But what? He's their dad, I know. I would just hate to see you get hurt again. You know, being a parent is a serious thing—I think you know that. I don't think Tom does."

"Well, I don't know," I say. I don't know what to say. It's nothing I haven't said to myself a thousand times, but to hear it from someone else, I wonder if I've been too hard on Tom, or too free about my feelings, in my conversations.

I get defensive. "Well, what do you know about being a father anyway?"

"Not much, that's true," he says wiping down the bar. And then he does something I will never forget. He throws a notepad down in front of me on the bar. I look at him. "Read it," he says.

"What is it?"

"My journal from Ireland."

"Why do you want . . ."

"Just read it—the first ten or so pages—then we can talk about kids." I can tell from the look in his eyes, almost pleading with me to understand his perspective, that I shouldn't argue any further. I pick up the journal and begin to read.

Much of the beginning is very typical—went to Aran Islands, signed up for classes, am in love with a beautiful redhead kind of stuff. But something a few pages in catches me dead. A girl back in his hometown that he has written to and not received a response from has written to him that she is pregnant with their child. "I'm ecstatic," he writes. "I was shocked at first, but after thinking and talking, I realize that I am overjoyed by this news." When I finish reading the entry I look up at him. He looks at me, gestures me to continue reading and turns to take care of another customer. After reading about a tortuous 8,000-mile ride back to America, Hogan writes that he is in his hometown but that the girl won't see him. He thinks of things to say to her, like even though they aren't in love, they are friends and can do this together. I am impressed by his attitude. In the end, though, the girl opts for an abortion, and Hogan is devastated. He never got a chance to talk to her. But it's not reading this in the journal that touches me as much as looking up to see Hogan sitting on the steps wiping tears away. The man who yelled at poor Ally only minutes ago to take a "fucking table," was now weeping in front of me.

I have no idea what to say, but sit down next to him and hold him around his shoulders. "I really wanted to have that kid," he whispers.

"I know," I say, "but maybe she just wasn't ready."

"I know," he says, wiping his eyes. At this moment, more than anything, I want to be with him. I still don't understand why he wanted me to know that about him, but this experience makes me want to love him. I suddenly understand his joy in taking my kids to the movies and wanting to hang out with us. But does he like the kids or me?

We don't talk much after that and I leave to pick up the kids, but not without giving him a hug before I go. My heart pounds during the embrace, but as we separate he says, "I can still see down your shirt, Kennedy." He smiles and touches my face and I playfully slap it away.

"Pervert," I call out before heading out the door.

Fourteen

For the next four weeks, I spend eight hours of every day learning more than I ever wanted to know about the bank: how to sell credit cards and how to get people to take their credit cards back. I learn the computer system, which despite my horrid phobia, I turn out to be quite good at. I have hated computers since high school. Computer classes in my high school were for the kids who would become administrative assistants or other administrative types, not for those who planned on going to prestigious colleges and changing the world, like me. Computers were horrible boxes with black backgrounds and orange writing.

But here at the bank I learn how to click between windows and send messages and e-mail, and I am so good at it that they put me in charge of some of the older ladies who haven't quite caught on yet.

When the four weeks of training are through, we are sent to the "floor." A football-field-size room full of cubicles. I have been sent to Dilbert-world. I have a computer and desk of my own. The most disturbing thing about the job is the sheer amount of information that my computer contains about the people I call. In addition to their addresses and phone numbers, I know their credit ratings, their social security numbers— even their mother's maiden name. I have, of course, been fingerprinted for security purposes, and I know I won't do anything with all of this information, but it still makes me feel uneasy. Our fingerprints, we are told, will be sent to Washington, D.C., where presumably the FBI will check them against their database to make sure we do not have felony criminal records.

The funny thing is, even through all of my uneasiness, I am very good at my job. I sit in my Customer Retention cubicle each day, scanning my computer screens, headphones permanently affixed to my head and waiting for my customers to answer their phones.

"Hello?" A tentative voice answers.

"Good morning, ma'am," I say. "This is Michelle from your bank, and I'm just calling to find out why you decided to give up your platinum card."

"Well, uh . . . I," the voice stammers through excuses. "You charged me late fees when I was only late once in ten years and then you all were rude to me on the phone."

"Did we do that?" My voice sounds shocked, although I am not in the slightest. Taking on a hint of Southern Belle, I proceed to clean up the damage.

"Oh my goodness—the computer says that we did do that, and I am just so sorry. Let me fix that for you and tell you what, between you and me, I'll drop your interest rate to 2.9 percent. Would that help you decide to take the card back?" At this point, I am out of my seat, walking as far as my headphone cord will let me and gesturing wildly with my hands. I am in my element.

"Really? You can do that?" Got her. I check her off my list and sign her up. You bet I can do that. I can do just about anything if it means the person on the other end of the phone will take back their credit card.

I sit back down in my cubicle and wait for the computer to dial up another victim. All day long I talk to people who have given up their credit cards in a noble effort to whittle down their debt or those who were angered by customer service or just had enough cards already. There are people with medical bills and with college tuition and none of this matters to me because I have one goal in mind: to sign them back up. That is my sole duty, for I am a customer retentionist.

On my very first call, I remembered everything I was supposed to mention, from the new lower rate we were supposed to offer to the free gift for signing back up with us. I was so congenial and so friendly that my guy not only signed up, but he thanked me for my wonderful work and asked to speak to my supervisor so that he could tell her what a great job I had done. I received a company commendation certificate, similar to the ones I was awarded in junior high school for being in the band, to hang in my very own cubicle.

Getting a commendation on your first call was unheard of, and I became an instant star. The rush was almost more than I could handle. Within days, I was an addict, constantly in search of the thrill of nailing a sale. I talked to all kinds of people. I validated their concerns. I apologized for our previous ineptness. I listened, which is the secret to sales. Most people just wanted to vent to someone. They wanted to tell me why their credit card payments were too high and how they didn't have enough money and how they were tired of people calling them at dinnertime.

I was God. I fixed it all. I rearranged payments. I moved around due dates. I promised to put notations in their file saying "don't call at 5:00 P.M." I didn't always put them in, but I promised I would.

"You've got this strange glaze over your face," Hogan says to me one night at O'Hara's. I have just had a particularly successful day getting customers in the three-months-old database, three months since they had given up their cards to take their cards back. I have also just been promoted for the first time—I am shocked that it has only taken a week—and I am in a my-job-is-great groove.

My promotion enables me to move my desk to the more veteran section of the customer retention floor and take on the six-months-old database. It's a Friday and the kids ask if they can stay at Diane's and finish the movie they are watching, please, please, please. And of course I cave, so I decide since it has been almost a whole week since I have been to O'Hara's, I will stop in for a soda and say hello.

"What glaze, Hogan?" I ask. We get right back into the groove—the insulting groove—easily.

"The glaze—the happy I'm alive and work for the credit card company glaze," he says.

"Well, it's not mixing drinks anymore, but it's a decent job, and I can't beat the benefits." I am trying to be cheerful and keep things light. If I let his remarks get me down, I'll never get past them, and then I'll feel worse. It is hard to hear this because I have been having my own doubts about the place recently. But Matt just started school, and Lydia and Alex are at Diane's during the day, so I don't want to mess with their schedule—again. Besides, work's just work, right?

"No, I know. I'm sorry . . . I just don't want to see you turn into one of them . . ."

"Oh my God, somebody note the date and time—Barb get me a pencil! Hogan just apologized to me!"

"Cute," he says, obviously hurt, a little too obviously if you ask me. It looks like he might have been drinking for a while, so I don't want to get him in some maudlin drunken state. We've talked a lot since the day I read his journal, but only across the bar. Diane says I should step it up and go out with him, but I'm afraid. Besides, I am technically still married since I can never seem to get Tom to sign all the right papers at all the right times. He has also recently just started showing up at the apartment whenever he feels like it, and I can never say no to the kids when they are so excited to see him. But it's beginning to piss me off. I want there to be designated visitation days and I want full custody, but I don't know how to accomplish this yet.

"Hey, what if we go to a movie?" I ask Hogan, all of a sudden. The quickness with which such an idea came out of my mouth shocks even me. "Yeah. The kids are at Diane's for the night and we could have, like, a real date, Hogan—what do you say?"

He looks shocked by my sudden offer. I know he and Jane are still living together, but I also know that things have gotten progressively worse. A girl at work said she saw her kissing someone in the parking lot. A guy from "upstairs." I also know that Hogan suspects it—he's said so a million times.

"I don't know . . ."

"What d'ya mean ya don't know. We've been hanging around each other for months—it's about time we went on a real date. I'm still dressed decently from work. My kids are fine. I haven't been out on a date in ages. C'mon Hogan, humor me, would ya?"

"Yeah, OK. No, that's a great idea. I'm hungry, though. Can we eat first?"

We sit at one of the tables upstairs in the dining room, and Ally waits on us, nervously. I tell her not to worry, that Hogan's really a wuss underneath all that hair and she laughs, spilling his mandatory Guinness on the table. She practically runs away.

"God, you have an amazing effect on people," I say.

"If she can't serve correctly, she shouldn't be working here," he says.

"Well, thank God you aren't in charge of firing the waitstaff—there'd be no one left. Even I have spilled an occasional drink."

"You shouldn't have told me that."

"Oh, shut up."

We fight like we've been married for twenty years already. I'm not sure if this is a good thing or not. I change the subject and ask a million "tell me your life story" questions. I already know about Ireland and his ex-wife, but I know nothing about where he grew up, if he has brothers, sisters, parents who are still alive. And I fill him in on the basics about me. He is surprised to learn about my working in Washington and going to American. People always are—they always wonder how a kid with so much potential could turn out . . . well, homeless and living in her car with the three kids she had when she was too young. So, I tell him most of the rest. Most of what he doesn't know from our previous conversations—the stuff I hold back, that I am too embarrassed about. It comes out easily with him.

We skip the movie and hang out at O'Hara's, which is as comfortable as a living room for us, and it's now empty except for the perpetual Scrabble tournament. I sit behind the bar on a cooler, drinking a screwdriver. He drinks a Guinness. And he begins to talk. About me. About us. The most amazing, poetically strange stuff I have ever heard.

"Everyday I would see you, walking around town with your tribe, and I would just want to be with you and protect you and keep you safe. Goddamnit, I have loved you since the first moment I saw you when you walked into the bar. I love watching you and the kids walk around town, and I always wanted to be with you. Damn it, you have to know that already."

I did not know that, actually. I was quite surprised to hear such an outpouring of emotion from a man who seemed so impenetrable on the exterior. Ever since I saw that ring on his finger, I have had no such thoughts of love with Hogan. Even after my birthday, when he said what he thought of me, I have pushed it out of my mind. A great friend, yes, but love? It never crossed my mind. Well, it crossed, but it never stuck. Not really.

"I have thought about you almost every minute since we met," he says. "That first day, when you walked in the bar, right before you came in, I got a shiver up my spine, like something was about to happen, and then there you were."

I am silent. Speechless. I have no idea how to respond. I cradle my drink and sip it slowly, listening, thinking.

"I don't know what to say," I say. We notice Lyle is getting ready to kick us out.

"Do you want to go somewhere?" he asks.

"Um—sure," I say. I am nervous. Scared. Not of him. Of what I'll feel. I don't want to be in love again. Not yet. Not this soon. But I can't not go with him. He has held all of this in for so long, it seems. And I want to hear more.

We walk out the door into a cool evening breeze. He leads me to his Jeep. We drive down to the bay. It seems so long since I spent my evenings here. We lean on the hood of the car, and he kisses me. Strong and full of more love and passion than I have ever tasted in my life. All at once it hits me. Him. And I want him more than anything. We pull at each other. He starts to take off my shirt, but a spotlight is over us. The police have caught us—two overgrown teenagers groping in the dark. They laugh and drive away. We laugh hysterically. And tentatively begin again. My nervousness completely subsides. I am in the moment. My mind a blank except for kissing, feeling this man.

"We have to stop," he says.

"Why?" I keep kissing him.

"It's almost 4:00 A.M. Misha, we can't do this here," he says, stroking my hair. "Not yet."

"You could come home with me." When did I become a temptress? Five hours ago, I had no idea he even had feelings for me, and now I am inviting him home?

He does take me home, but he leaves me at the door. In his gentle squeeze on the back of my neck I can feel all of the love he has held for me surging through me, engulfing me.

"We have to figure this out," he says. "We have to do this slowly."

At least he is using his head.

I lay down in bed, rather glad that the children aren't here because I am shaking with all the passion of the evening. The shock of being loved and not knowing it. Wondering if I feel the same. My stomach hurts with the pain of not knowing—or is it the pain of his not being here?

I fall asleep and when I wake up, it's all there again. I go to Diane's and have breakfast with the kids before work. My stomach is in knots. I go to work with my stomach in knots. I can't eat. I have no idea what all of this means. I want to call him. But I can't. I call during lunch, and I hang up when he answers. I know he knows it's me. I am confused by my feelings and confused by his sudden remoteness. Why isn't he beating my door down? Does he regret that he said anything at all?

After a couple of days of being apart, he appears at my door.

"We have to talk," he says.

"OK, sit down." I have since bought a kitchen table. The kids come in and stare at him, recognize who it is and then start jumping on him and showing him their toys.

"They like to show off when someone comes over," I say.

"Hi, guys. Hey, would you go play for a bit? Then we'll talk." The kids are satisfied with this and wander back into the living room.

"About the other night," he says.

"Yes?" I reach for his hands across the table and look at him with my mooniest of eyes.

"It was a mistake."

"Oh." I am not expecting this, especially after how vehemently he pursued me.

"I mean, I do love you, but I'm with Jane, and this just isn't right. Is it?"

"So if you love me and I'm pretty sure I love you, then what's not right?"

"You love me?"

"I just said so, didn't I?"

"I don't know," he says, resting his chin on his chest. "I don't know what to do. Jane and I live together. Do you know how hard it is to break up when you're already this far?"

"Um . . . yeah," I say.

"Oh . . . yeah," he says.

"Look," I say, suddenly feeling quite confident, "I don't know what to tell you. But you said some pretty powerful things the other night, and I felt some pretty powerful things, and if they're only half true, then I think we have a chance at something really special."

"Yeah?"

"Yeah." And then I start to cry. I can't help it, it just starts to pour out of me. "I just think . . . I don't know. I think I might really love you and now you're going to go and leave and . . ."

But he stops me and walks over to where I'm sitting. We stand up and hold each other, both of us crying, until the kids walk in and look at us like we're insane.

Then, like a madman he says he has to go and break up with Jane.

"It will be a long night," he says. "Can I come back here when I'm done?"

"Of course." Part of me believes he won't come back.

But at 2:00 A.M., there he is, a guitar on his back and a backpack in his hand. I let him in and he puts his stuff down in the kitchen.

"Come sit on the steps with me," he says. "I need a smoke."

I shut the door behind me, but he goes back and opens it. "So we can hear the kids," he says.

We sit on the stoop by the third floor door and we talk about how horribly things went with Jane. I talk about my impending divorce—only fifty dollars in Maine if you do it yourself, I joke.

"I should get one of those too," he says.

"A divorce?" I ask. "Oh, yeah, you're still married too, aren't you?"

"Yup."

"But I thought still being married is what kept you from getting married again." He puts his arm around me and kisses me.

"It's what kept me from marrying Jane . . ."

"Oh, no," I say. "We are not getting married."

"We'll see . . ."

We go inside and make love for the first time on my sleeping bag on the floor bed. After, he plays the guitar that I didn't know he could play while I drift off to sleep. In the morning—entirely too early considering we fell asleep as the sun came up—we wake up with Lydia sleeping between us.

Hogan suddenly just lives with us. At least until Jane can find another place, and he can move back into his house. I am determined to take things slow, and he is determined to make sure I know he's not trying to take advantage. He gives me the entire month's rent (why couldn't we have been roommates a month ago?) and he is always buying food for the kids. I'd complain about having too many boxes of Twinkies around, but who am I to complain about free food? Hogan continues to make fun of my job, but I persevere, hoping that one day I can get out of retention and into computer education or public relations. I file for my divorce and go to court—alone. Tom doesn't show up, and the judge awards me custody of the children.

I continue to get promoted at work and the kids seem to adjust well to Hogan being around. It's as if he was always there. I keep trying to have little talks with them and explain it all to them. They nod and happily run off to play. There is no animosity between them and Hogan. I wonder if it's because they too learned to like him as a friend first.

Tom has started to come around less and less. I have never understood him, I realize, and have finally stopped trying. I let him see the kids when he does come by, and I don't let him make promises he won't keep. He stops babysitting, which is just as well, because the kids prefer going to Diane's.

One Saturday, I have to work a half-day and Diane is out of town. Hogan volunteers to sit with the kids.

"No problem," he says.

"No problem," Matt and Lyd say.

"OK," I say, "but call me if you need anything." I figure Hogan—I still can't call him John, it sounds strange coming out of my mouth—has gotten the routine down by now.

It's the day of Princess Diana's funeral and I am to sell more people their credit cards back. As I make my calls, I can hear their TVs on in the background. Everyone is watching the funeral. One woman is so upset that she repeats the agreement we have to make them say back to me through tears, doing anything she can to get me off the phone. I don't care though. I just write her name down on my list and make another call.

But somehow, Hogan and my own conscience have gotten

through. It could just be that his voice is still ringing in my head because he just called to inform me that while he innocently went to the bathroom, Alex pushed the VCR off the TV, and it is now broken.

"But don't worry," he says, "We're going to buy you another one, right now."

Whatever it is, I am suddenly watching myself make these phone calls, and I don't like what I see. As the computer dials, I am struck by thoughts of, "Is this what I should be doing with my life?" "Would my children be proud of how their mother spends her day?" "Do I want my kids to do this when they grow up just because it pays decently and has a 401K?"

How many nights had Hogan sat beside me and asked me what I really wanted to do with my life? I told him I wanted to open a bar that had a bookstore in it—a good idea, he thought. Or, I said, I wanted to write. "Making a living out of writing," he said, "is like trying to be a rock star."

But the steadiness of the bank kept me coming back. On this day, however, something is wrong. I can't focus.

The last straw is a particularly ruthless twenty minutes I spend at the end of my shift talking to a woman who had given up her card because of her medical bills. After a nice conversation during which I am only half listening to what she is saying because I am waiting for my opening to sell her back her card, she tells me that ever since she was diagnosed with inoperable cancer, she has been trying to reduce the debt she will leave behind. Still, this is not enough to sequester my desire to sell. I am an addict, and I will do anything to mark another name off my list.

I am about to regale this poor woman with a tale of a lower interest rate designed to make her debt load easier when I catch myself looking around the room. The glaze. Hogan was right. I tell the woman that she certainly doesn't need this card or any other. I also tell her that I don't even have a credit card, and then we spend the rest of my shift talking about the evils of credit card companies and doctors. Big Brother tapes every call, and so I am sure that this one is on the top of the list for the next staff meeting, but it doesn't matter.

I go home and tell Hogan I quit my job, I think. I call in sick the next day, but I don't go back.

Fifteen

Pink. It's pink. I'm not surprised. I expected as much. I walk out into the kitchen. I've been sick lately, a telltale sign for me. The kids are outside playing. It's now late October, and we have lived in Hogan's house for a couple of weeks. He has eleven acres and a large house out in Searsmont. It's getting colder, and it's nice to be near a fireplace again. There is a lot of room for the kids to run and they don't have to share a bedroom.

It was hard leaving the apartment, but Mrs. Hopkins understood and easily let me out of my lease. With all the new people in town working for the bank, it was easy for her to find a new renter.

Lyle gives me my job back, but I am only working part-time. My goal now is to save for a pub of our own.

But there it is. Pink.

Hogan is outside, talking with my parents. They have come up to see the house. I feel good presenting them with a normal life for us once again. We are beginning to heal our relationship—the one I have trounced on because of my inconsistent life and constant need. I peek around the front door and ask Hogan to come inside and help me with some drinks for the children. I don't want my parents to hear. I have no idea what they will think. Certainly not surprised, but surely disappointed. But I'm not. I'm as happy as I've ever been.

"I'm pregnant," I say as soon as he walks into the kitchen. He says nothing but jumps up and down waving his hands around. It's a humorous sight—this grown, large, sometimes grumpy, passionate man is actually giddy. He begins to cry and for the fortieth time asks me to marry me. I'm still refusing, after all our conversations about never getting married again, I don't want to be a hypocrite, but I don't know how much longer I can hold out.

In my mind we are already married, having exchanged silver rings bought in a tourist shop in Haverhill and reciting ad lib vows on the banks of Penobscot Bay.

Tom is around sometimes. He visits the kids occasionally, but has removed himself to a life on his land. I'll never know if it was having a family that was too much for him, or just me. I'll never know why he just let us walk out of his life; but slowly, I am beginning not to care so much. Strangely, the children don't talk about him. Alex is permanently attached to Hogan's hip. They feel complete, I think. Secure, I'm sure.

I never hear from the bank. No one ever calls to see if I died, but miraculously another paycheck is deposited into my checking account. And then another. Every other week for three months. I call and tell them over and over, but they tell me that I am wrong, that this couldn't possibly be happening. Far be it from me to disagree with policy. I keep the money and am blissfully jobless for a while. It's like winning the lottery.

Epilogue

W riting this book, six years after the fact, it's odd to think that I was homeless. Granted, I was really only a passing visitor to the vast land that is homelessness. I never lived in a cardboard box. Or a homeless shelter. I never had to deal with real danger, like drugs being around the children or drive-by shootings or some of the things that make homelessness a terrifying existence for many people. I never had to sleep outside in the winter like the man who slept on the Capitol Building steps when I was a page in D.C., although that cabin in Maine was awfully close. If you have to live out of your car, Stone Harbor was a damn fine place to do it.

But there is something about being at the bottom—at the bottom of the bottom—that never quite leaves you. All of a sudden, even with a good job and great kids and a great husband—yes, I married him—you become acutely aware of that one paycheck, which separates you from the car apartment. And I will never get over it. I will never forget what it was like to drive home and be home all at the same time. I will never forget the feeling of being so absolutely alone, with three babies totally dependent on every move I made.

And yes, I now appreciate having a house and a phone and electricity. The kids, for their part, remember very little. Matthew and Lydia remember the apartment in Stone Harbor, and they remember our noisy car, but they were surprised to hear how long we actually slept in it. They remember the beach and the pub. And they remember the heat. But they don't remember that a diet of ramen noodles was necessarily bad. In fact, they still ask for them all the time.

In the meantime, we found our way to Wisconsin, where Hogan had gone to college. He ended up working with computers—a talent I didn't know he possessed—and for the Packers, a team one must learn to love if one is going to be allowed to stay in Green Bay. A stay-at-home mom again, I found my way to writing through the Internet and then, as Alex and Liam (the baby of the family) got older, to the local newspaper. I also found a way to calm down a little and give things, like careers, time before I give up on them.

Now, after five happy years in Wisconsin, we have recently made our way back east, to purchase my parents' farm in Vermont. So I have come full circle; at least, I hope that's what it is. I don't know if it's true that you can't go home again. Maybe not. But maybe you can make a new life in a familiar place.

According to The National Coalition for the Homeless, as of 2000, 1.2 million children are homeless on any given night. Supporting this figure are estimates from the U.S. Department of Education that report almost 400,000 homeless children were served by the nation's public schools last year. Since more than half of all homeless children are under the age of six and not yet in school, a minimum of 800,000 children can be presumed to be homeless.

Families are the fastest growing segment of the homeless population, now accounting for almost 40 percent of the nation's homeless. More than 85 percent of homeless families are headed by single mothers, with the average homeless family comprised of a young mother and her two young children, most of whom are below the age of six. Homeless mothers have an average annual income of under $8,000, living at 63 percent of the federal poverty level for a family of three.

In 2002, The Snapshot Survey of the Homeless, released by the Association of Gospel Rescue Missions (AGRM) showed that the current economic slowdown is having a significant effect on our nation's homeless and poor. Nearly 60 percent of the more than 20,000 homeless people surveyed nationwide say it is harder for them to find work today than it was six months ago, and more than a third (37 percent) of those responding indicated that they were homeless, at least in part, due to economic conditions.

The report also showed a dramatic increase among homeless families coming to Rescue Missions. Intact families—husband and wife and children—accounted for 25 percent of the families served, up from 17 percent in 2001, and the largest percentage ever noted among that group in the fourteen-year history of the survey.

These are staggering figures to me. And it is compounded when I learn that while some people who become homeless have spiraled downward through drug or alcohol abuse or other "less savory" issues, some are just plain old people—like me, or maybe even you. Even now, as I write this, I am a good couple of paychecks away from being there again, but not so far from it that it isn't scary. But I won't go there again. I will do whatever it takes to keep my family and myself from being there again and fortunately, I have a partner who feels the same.

There is so much help available for people without homes or without food that it absolutely shocks me. I had no idea. I had no idea that if I had just walked my agnostic self into a church I could have received help. Almost any church. Since that time, I have also heard of other organizations that can help, like the Salvation Army, the American Red Cross, and a host of local organizations across the country that help battered women, victims of abuse, or those who need food or housing assistance. Unfortunately (or perhaps fortunately), very few of these organizations are government related.

Looking back, I wish I had had the interest to learn if there were other homeless people in Stone Harbor. I'm sure there must have been. But I was selfish and so totally focused on us that I lacked the desire to find out. I wish I could have spent time with some people who really understood when I say that it costs more to be poor than to be rich. I wish I had taken advantage of programs I learned about much later, like child care assistance and food pantries and security deposit assistance. But no one prepares you for those things when they are sending you off to the real world.

It's hard to accept help when you need it. What's harder is never being offered it.

A couple of years ago, I told my story to a friend. I hadn't talked about it much until then. Not many people, including my parents (except for those I worked with and Hogan) were aware of the extent of my desperation. I'm such a cheerful person that it often shocks people to learn of this "darkness" in my past. This friend was beyond shocked. She couldn't believe

I had "survived." Until that moment, it hadn't occurred to me that I had "survived" anything. I just did it. I went to work. Made money. Did the best I could.

My children are happy, healthy, and intelligent children. They are not greedy. They are normal kids, who want normal things, but somehow, without them knowing it, they have learned from the experience. They do not judge friends by who has the best toys or video game system. They appreciate a day on the lake as much as, if not more than, a day at the amusement park. They understand when I say, "I can't afford it." They have never, ever been fooled into thinking that there is a money tree in the backyard.

I wish I had learned these lessons as early as they have. I have yet to learn some of them.

Matt, for his part, is a regular twelve-year-old. He loves to read, play sports, and hang out with his friends. He loves the Green Bay Packers and is a little upset that we moved away from Wisconsin, but he has many new friends and I'm sure he'll get through it. He is clever and funny and excruciatingly smart. He puts my hard-earned math skills to shame and is wise beyond his years in many ways.

Lydia, who is now eleven, continues to be fearless. I don't know if she fully comprehends the brushes with death that she has had and it makes her more fearless than she might have been otherwise, but whatever the reason, she likes to scare me by standing up on the top of jungle gyms and racing her skateboard down hills. With three brothers, I'm afraid she didn't have a lot of time to be a real "girly" girl, but she can hold her own as a tomboy. She loves our new farm and is looking forward to snowboarding. She was also instrumental in our family's purchase of our first dog since Hogan came into our lives. Hogan, knowing the trauma Lydia went through, gave up his beloved Astro in order to accommodate us. We now have a gangly, yet very gentle, Chesapeake Bay Retriever named Gatsby who loves Lydia (and the rest of us) immensely.

Alex, at eight, is our artist and in truth, remembers nothing about life before Hogan. John has always been his dad, and he understands little about our time in the car. He is a happy and rambunctious second grader.

Liam is now six and is the last of the tribe. He, too, calls Hogan, John, and in our house, John is just another word for Dad. In fact, Liam once watched a cartoon where a little girl was missing her father and said, "Oh, she misses her John."

John doesn't mind not being called Dad so much, mostly because when the kids—all of them—introduce him to their friends they say, "This is my dad, John."

As for Tom, there isn't much to say. He's just not a part of our lives. I've told the kids they can write or call him whenever they want, but they have never asked. I asked Matt and Lydia what they think about him and they said, "We don't want to see him. We just don't think about him at all unless you mention it. He is not a part of our life anymore." And that's fine for now. That may change some day, but right now they have school and friends and sports and Christmas lists on their minds.

Tom did visit them twice while we lived in Wisconsin, but he has not been heard from since. He has not remembered birthdays or holidays, and the kids do not look for things in the mail. He is living, I think, the life he wanted. A life on the land, with a new wife and a homemade home.

"What do you tell your kids about that time?" my friend asked me.

It's simple really. I tell them the truth. There was a time, after Lydia's accident, when I couldn't afford a place to live. We had to sleep in the car for a few months. But we spent a lot of time at the beach and it wasn't so bad. That's where we met Hogan. And if it had not been for that time, we would have never had Liam.

"Why didn't you give your kids up for adoption?" she asked me. She wasn't trying to be cruel. She really wanted to know. I tried not to take offense. But honestly, it never crossed my mind. Never. Not one time in all of those months did I think, "Oh, I'll just call up the government and have them place my children with other families. Then I won't have to worry about it anymore." I still can't think it, even as I write the words. We were a team. We are a team. I do nothing without my children, my family. Living in the car was a mere bump in the road and although it occurred to me plenty of times that we might never have a "real" house, it never occurred to me that we would be homeless forever. My brain just doesn't work that way, I guess. I'm always looking ahead to the next bend in the road. Although, as I've gotten older, I've learned not to take quite so many of the turns.

Sometimes I wonder if I should have stayed on my own, remained alone for a while longer. But I look at my children and know that I made the right choice. Some may say that I gave up, that I thought I couldn't make it without a man, but I know that's untrue. Because I did make it on my own. I found my apartment, held my job, fed my kids, and eventually found my purpose. I just got lucky and found love too. So what if it all happened in the same year?